Building (in) the Future

Building (in) the Future
Recasting Labor in Architecture

Peggy Deamer and Phillip G. Bernstein,
editors

Yale School of Architecture, New Haven
Princeton Architectural Press, New York

Published by
Princeton Architectural Press
37 East Seventh Street
New York, New York 10003
www.papress.com

Yale School of Architecture
P.O. Box 208242
New Haven, Connecticut 06511
www.architecture.yale.edu

Support for this publication
was provided to the Yale School
of Architecture by Autodesk, Inc.

Yale School of Architecture
Publications Director
Nina Rappaport

Yale School of Architecture
Assistant Managing Editor
Zachary R. Heineman

Princeton Architectural Press
Editors
Nancy Eklund Later
Carolyn Deuschle

Graphic Designer
Jeff Ramsey

The editors would like to thank
Dean Robert A.M. Stern and
Autodesk, Inc., for their support.
Without them, this book would
not have been possible. We
would also like to thank Assistant
Dean John Jacobson and Events
Coordinator Richard DeFlumeri,
both of whom provided essen-
tial administrative support.
Additional thanks go to the
contributors and their respective
publication assistants.
P.D. & P.B.

Library of Congress
Cataloging-in-Publication Data

Building (in) the future :
recasting labor in architecture
/ Peggy Deamer and Phillip
Bernstein, editors.
p. cm.
ISBN 978-1-56898-806-1
(alk. paper)
1. Architectural practice.
2. Architects and builders.
3. Interprofessional relations.
I. Deamer, Peggy. II. Bernstein,
Phillip (Phillip Gordon), 1957–
III. Title: Recasting labor in
architecture. IV. Title: Building
the future.
NA1995.B85 2009
720–dc22
                    2009029521

In memory of Robert Gutman (1926–2007), a most sensitive analyzer of the architectural profession and the design process, who was at the center of discussions that led to the formulation of this book.

Collaboration

Foreword
Andrew Ross

By the early 1970s, when John Turner and Richard Fichter published their influential edited volume of planning essays, *Freedom to Build,* a third of the world's population was housing itself with its own hands, often in the absence of government and professional intervention and sometimes in spite of it.[1] In the United States, as many as 160,000 families annually, they noted, were building their own homes. In part, this was to minimize costs by making the most efficient use of handyman know-how. But Turner, as a good anarchist, was also inclined to believe that ordinary people perceived building to be a path to empowerment. His lionization of the self-build movement, which originated in his experience with the self-housing efforts of poor Peruvians in the late 1950s, would eventually be propagated worldwide under the auspices of the World Bank's Transport and Urban Development Department. This self-build spirit was further reflected in the returning appreciation of communal architecture, summarized in Bernard Rudofsky's 1964 Museum of Modern Art exhibition Architecture without Architects, and soon after fed into the advocacy planning movement of the late 1960s. Each of these initiatives posed a serious challenge to the professional self-image of the omniscient design expert. Architects, these mavericks argued, should dictate less and listen more, learning as much as possible from a building's end user. Ideally they should view their role as assisting dwellers to house themselves: after all, *housing* is a verb, as Turner himself liked to say.

Forty years later, the architect's role in building in the United States is diminished, but not because more people are building their own houses. These days merchant builders dominate the industry, using formulaic plans that are much more likely to have been drawn up by lawyers than by architects. And so architects are conspicuously absent from the vast majority of building projects in the United States (from 90 to 95 percent, in the most apocryphal of estimates), their involvement now limited to the luxury housing niche or to the signature realm of public institutional landmarks and brand-conscious corporate towers. Ironically, as the practical influence of architects over the built landscape has dwindled, the cultural power of select high-profile designer names has skyrocketed. The bestowal of such a name as Viñoly, Gehry, Nouvel, Rogers, Piano, Foster, Hadid, Calatrava, or Koolhaas on an idiosyncratic building is now the anchor around which city managers try to engineer cultural districts for the much-sought-after "creative class," boosting land value in all adjacent neighborhoods. Developing countries scramble to commission these wonderstuff

1   Cited in Jeff Lustig, "The Mixed Legacy of Clark Kerr: A Personal View," *Academe* 90, no. 4 (Jul.–Aug. 2004).

names in order to showcase the global ambitions of their catch-up economies. In the meantime, fewer and fewer trained architects are finding opportunities to earn their livelihood out of their profession.

There is nothing paradoxical about this situation. It is a familiar product of our neoliberal times, when the top dogs increasingly live in a different world from the rest of us. The forces of deregulation have decoupled the old relationship between commissioning state agencies and the architectural profession, allowing speculators and other entrepreneurs to intervene and directly influence bids and contracts. So, too, is the commercial subcontracting system of the merchant builders now fully protected by legal codes and zoning regulations that favor powerful interests in the building industries. Architects willing to challenge these legal constraints, as the New Urbanists have done, face opprobrium from the gatekeepers of capital-A Architecture for compromising the profession's devotion to aesthetic innovation. Liberalization has also seen the rise of branding and other value-adding devices that position intellectual property at the core of the new service-driven economy. The outcome for architects is a winner-takes-all system where a small number of feted practitioners compete for the jackpot.

The rise of subcontracting on a global scale has meant that routine design operations—drafting, rendering, modeling—are increasingly assigned to cheaper labor in offshore locations. There are few architectural firms in which high-skill jobs are not threatened by this rise up the value ladder of outsourcing. In the meantime the bulk of the actual labor going into the built environment is increasingly performed by undocumented migrants, whose own housing needs and life aspirations are as invisible to the architectural profession as they are to the general public. Indeed, given the explosion in the number of manufactured homes—by far the biggest growth sector in the housing industry—it is only a matter of time before prison labor (which currently accounts for a small proportion of manufactured production) becomes as indispensable to the industry as immigrant labor.

Ideally, any comprehensive analysis of the labor economy of architecture ought to take account of the involvement of dweller-builders, trade artisans, and unskilled construction workers. Arguably, it should also include the work of public participants in charrettes, impact hearings, crowdsourcing, and, above all, the focus groups conducted by the industry's market researchers. Why? Because the massive, ongoing effort to transfer work from the realm of production to that of the consumer is an increasingly vital hidden labor component of consumer capitalism. The labor of all these nonpedigreed actors is an important part of the story, but one that is seldom mentioned in debates within the profession. And architecture, as it is taught and represented in the academy, is very much an insider's profession.

Except, perhaps, during the 1960s, the profession has been less subject to challenges to its monopoly of expertise from outsiders or laypersons than have professions such as medicine, law, or religion. A chief reason for this is architecture's confirmed detachment from the labor of fabrication, not to mention the vigorous activities of the end user. The gentlemanly ideal of distance from the business of production—an essential component of the architectural profession's self-image—has persisted against all odds. It survived the early-twentieth-century era of the factory ethos, preached as an avant-garde imperative by the likes of Corbusier and the Bauhaus school and widely adopted as a corporate model in the process-flow organization of large design firms at midcentury. The ideal underwent a renovation at the hand of boosters of the postindustrial concept of flexible specialization who imagined that a new life lay ahead for the "mysteries of craft." Most of all, it has endured in the teeth of dangers posed by advanced technologies of design, whose capacity to "self-optimize" threatens to encroach even further on the autonomy of design functions that are left in control of the practicing architect.

This last scenario is the immediate occasion for this book. Computer-aided design (CAD) and computer numerical control (CNC) fabrication is now so advanced in its use of parametrics that the conception and execution of a building is more and more the result of computational programming. How has this affected the role of architects and their relationships with the other specialized professionals—engineers, technicians, general contractors, and project managers—involved in bringing a plan to realization? What does the new organization of labor among these professionals look like? Is the news good or bad, and for whom?

Like all technologies, knowledge-processing machines have the potential to be used either as artisanal tools or as efficiency instruments of industrialization. When employed as tools they are greeted as breakthroughs in the cause of innovation, while their deployment as industrial technologies is feared because it degrades and routinizes skills that lie at the heart of the self-reliant artisan's livelihood. Both of these responses have been widely aired in the debates within the profession about CAD. On the one hand, the new technologies are touted as an opportunity to expand the designer's ability to solve technical problems, to deliver accurate plans, and to exhaust every possible imaginative angle. On the other hand, defenders of the Ruskinian tradition of handicraft see the imminent demise of the profession in the spectacle of plans being calculated rather than drawn, as Kenneth Frampton implies in his essay. Proponents of a brave new world of design speak about modernizing the field and of fully maximizing the potential of the designer's hitherto-underutilized cognitive faculties. Forecast-ers of the death of architecture see automation as a de-skilling process and point to the devastation visited on other professions, like medicine by bureaucratic, metric-based technologies such as managed health care. Yet neither has much to say about the reorganization of labor within and around the design and building professions.

This volume is a first effort to address that topic. In its own way, it adds to the literature on labor process initiated by Harry Braverman's classic *Labor and Monopoly Capital: The Degradation of Work in the Twentieth Century* (1974), which tracks the manner in which industrialists introduce advanced technologies in order to reorganize the workplace for efficiency and control. Unlike most of the post-Braverman scholarly analyses, however, this book draws, with bold eclecticism, on the viewpoints of practitioners in a host of related professional fields. Readers of these manifold, often contradictory, contributions will build their own composite picture of where things stand, and it is almost certainly the case that they will take away differing interpretations.

Regardless, the chief achievement of this book is to estab-lish that the demarcation between design and fabrication is no longer feasible, if indeed it ever was. In these pages, the fully coop-erative, interdependent nature of the building enterprise stands revealed. The increasing complexity of infrastructural technologies alone has required general contractors and others on the technical side to take responsibility for design decisions. Design functions are more and more divided up and assigned to specialized loca-tions, many of them well outside the professional firm, and some of them deep within the artisanal trade structure. This also means, as Paolo Tombesi points out, that opportunities for architectural interns to move up from clerical to professional positions within a firm have been drastically reduced. As a result, graduates are just as likely to advance their career prospects by taking technical positions with building-trade subcontractors and gaining industrial experience as by relying on their design credentials. As Tombesi himself argues, the outcome of this and other related develop-ments is that, more and more, building needs to be thought of as a "branch of architecture, rather than keeping architecture a privileged but inward-looking subset of building."

If this shift in perspective is borne out, then it is character-istic of other professions as well. In the academy, for example, as former University of California president Clark Kerr once predicted, credentialed faculty now see themselves as tenants rather than as owners of their institutions.[2] Like most doctors and lawyers, they are managed employees, less and less in control of their vocational workplace and more and more regarded as providers of specific services. There is no doubt that we are witnessing a deformation of the professions—at least of the terms through which they were originally created—to establish a monopoly over knowledge fields and markets. Our siege mentality encourages us to imagine that the forces of commodification are closing in on our protected havens. This is an understandable delusion, but professionals and their institutions have ever been in the service of the interests of capital-owners. The difference today is that the professional services in question are now the source of the raw materials—ideas, images, symbols—of the burgeoning knowledge industries. The capacity of design, for example, to add value is emblematic of the new mode of accumulation that seeks to exploit neglected generators of profit. In this respect, design is too important to be left in the hands of professionals: capital's structural need to control this newly crucial domain requires that it be broken up and assigned to specialized nodes on a production chain. Greater efficiency may result, but that is not the primary goal. The chief motivation is to take control away from individuals vested, by tradition, with more responsibility and oversight than capital-owners would like.

It is not surprising, then, that advocates of the design-build movement—the most aggressive counterresponse to this new division of labor—promote their services to the public by promising greater efficiency and more authentic quality control. The iconography of the movement is irradiated with loving tributes to the venerable institution of the master builder, but its raison d'etre is firmly rooted in present conditions. Integrating design, engineering, and constructing under one roof (or in one executive team) may ensure more accountability over cost, quality, and schedule, but underlying this pragmatic appeal is an ongoing struggle, at once desperate and noble, to reclaim the profession's own freedom to build.

If this impulse to regain control is not to end up as a rearguard action, driven by a siege mentality, then its advocates might do well to recall the spirit of Turner's encomium about self-building, for his was a bottom-up version of the "architecture without architects" that is increasingly being practiced from the top down. The response to his call was not driven by fear at the prospect of deprofessionalization, which is the prevailing mood today. Rather, it was inspired by the challenge of reeducating the profession.

2   Cited in Clark Kerr, *The Uses of the University* (Cambridge, MA: Harvard University Press, 1963).

Preface
Robert A. M. Stern

The field of architecture has expanded and become increasingly complex in recent decades, perhaps most dramatically as a direct consequence of the new digital media and their impact on both the design and the physical realization of buildings.

The dramatic change that the digital age has brought to architecture is vividly apparent in the schools, where one rarely sees a Mayline or a roll of yellow trace on a student's desk. Triangles, French curves, and other tools that were the stock-in-trade of architects for hundreds of years are not only no longer in use, but also not even recognizable by many young designers. Instead, computers abound, not only for information gathering, written communication, and drafting, but also for the shaping of form—for initiating design.

Today's typical student enters the study of architecture largely through a virtual world, not through a systematic examination of physical relationships. Nonetheless, issues of dimension, heft, tactility, and materiality remain essential to architecture as built environment, no matter how tantalizing the "pixelated" world is.

In professional practice, coping with digitally enhanced technology in architecture has become a constant. As we absorb the impact of the computer into our discipline, let us not lose sight of the fact that since the dawn of the industrial age, each generation has had to harness the innovations of its time to the age-old task of shaping the built environment. The industrial age gave rise to a belief that craft and machine manufacture were locked in combat with each other, with seemingly no victor proclaimed. Now it just may be that the computer offers a means to end that battle. However ironic this may at first blush seem to be, such may just be the case. The computer has the potential to expand the professional's control over the world of built form by linking designers with constructors more closely than since the dawn of machine production, and we are beginning to recognize this. Indeed, we may now be entering an age of the master-builder-craftsman that John Ruskin sought to revive but getting there in a way Ruskin could not have anticipated. The expanding technology of computer software and digital fabrication techniques promises to make it possible for architects to regain their proper and responsible role not only with regard to design but also in the generation of construction documents and fabrication of the finished product.

The new digital paradigms promise an unprecedented level of collaboration among design professionals, fabricators, and others. But with that collaboration comes the possibility of great risk. Who ultimately controls the process of design and fabrication if so many can have direct access to the documents initiating and describing it? Who owns the ideas? The drawings? This book addresses these important questions and many more related to the emergence of new paradigms of design and performance. While we do not know where digitally supported professional collaboration will lead us in the future, we can but marvel at its potential as put forward here by a diverse group of professionals, artisans, and theorists, who in their daily work push the boundaries of the familiar, in addition to those who measure those leaps in light of the risks they involve—the construction managers, marketers, and lawyers.

There are many questions to ponder as architecture moves forward in the digital age, but one that should concern us above all asks whether it is architecture itself that must change or the way it is practiced, and if either must change, is that change to be evolutionary or revolutionary? In other words, will the new technologies free us to design buildings that are deemed better because they differ radically in form from what went before or because they more closely than ever before meet long-valued criteria of performance—or a little bit of both? Only with the passage of time will we know for sure that the future is in safe hands.

The promise of a new paradigm of integrated design and construction is reflected in the collaboration of this book's two editors: Peggy Deamer, who is an architect and theorist, Phillip Bernstein, who is an architect and a computer technologist. I would like to extend my thanks to them for editing this collection of essays. I would also like to thank the publication team at Princeton Architectural Press, especially Senior Acquisitions Editor Nancy Eklund Later and Assistant Editor Carolyn Deuschle; Yale School of Architecture Publications Director Nina Rappaport; Assistant Managing Editor Zachary R. Heineman ('09); and Graphic Designer Jeff Ramsey.

Introduction
Peggy Deamer

The subtle shift that occurred in architectural discourse around the year 2000, from formal concerns focusing on the blob to production concerns centering on digital fabrication, has proved to be more profound than anyone would have predicted. The emphasis on production and process over aesthetics and representation has changed the nature of our architectural horizons, both in theory and in practice. But for all the recent publications that promote the power of digital fabrication/parametric design and describe its potential for liberating our productive (and hence formal) horizons, none examine the effect of this on how we—designers, architects, builders—conceive of our *work*. This book examines not just the process of parametric design but the labor in that process; not just the power of technology but also its effect on technologically engaged subjects.

Although some philosophers, such as John Locke and Hannah Arendt, have made much of the distinction between labor and work—with *labor* addressing life's biological needs and *work* referring to rhetorical and worldly striving—it is not, for the most part (e.g., Frampton), the operative dichotomy in this text. We want to operate between and within the connotations of both words—the work that we all know we do when we "go to work" or "work out a problem," and also capitalism's "system of labor" that we as makers operate in and in which we struggle to reap the "fruits of our labor."

Here, the traditional definitions of designer, architect, and builder come under attack as the relationship of each to the other shifts. *Designer* is no longer equated with *architect*; fabricators, engineers, and software programmers can lay equal claim to authorial designation. The architect has access to all the economic/organizational parameters originally known only to the builder; hence, control of the critical path is mingled with control of form. But it should be emphasized that the new modes of production do not cause this shift; they further destabilize an existing dysfunctional and antagonistic relationship between all players in the client-architect-contractor trichotomy—a dysfunctionality that, being highly overdetermined and, like capital itself, highly self-contradictory, demands systemic change. This is the reason that the words *digital* and *parametric* do not appear in the title of this work: while new technology is at the center of all the essays in this book, it is treated here only as a catalyst to the larger issue of how the profession and all the players in it want and need to reposition themselves for the future.

This book began partly as an inquiry into why, just as production and not form became the new area of architectural concern, theory seemed to go into retreat. In academia, the theoretical position that accompanied the emergence of parametric design quickly became postcritical: an opportunity to stop critical thought and just start making things. Why get hung up on the issues of co-option and hegemonic culture when we can have so much fun participating in and adding to the goods? But it seemed, and still seems, in fact, that theory could and should be more interesting and more important than ever: more interesting because it finally had something—production and its economic viability—to chew on, and important because theory above all should not retreat just as labor, new technology, and money enter the picture. The intellectual inquiry moved from this observation to an examination of how architecture as a profession does indeed officially and unofficially organize its labor.

The other impetus for this book was exasperation felt by those at the vanguard of the profession with the protocols, both contractual and self-imposed, limiting our ability to exchange information and share expertise across professional boundaries. Contracts memorializing business practices designed to limit liability, already having shown themselves to increase antagonism and constrain design's social reach, had been clearly proved to be impediments to disciplinary empowerment. Likewise, the traditional organization of the architectural office—linear, hierarchical, and star driven—while still intact, was and is increasingly nonsensical. What was necessary from the professional point of view was not only the revision of standard contracts but a conceptual reclassification of the players.

Thus, for the purposes of this inquiry, theory was irrelevant without practice, and practice, impoverished without theory.

The book is divided into two sections, "Working and Making" and "Collaboration." The first explores the relationship between the maker and the object and, within this, between design (involving form, representation, and space) and craft (involving materials and tools) and between human and technological production. The second section explores the relationships between the makers— architects, builders, subcontractors, fabricators—and, within this, between intention and execution, thinking and making, opportunity and liability, and innovation and responsibility. Both sections also keenly investigate how digital technology disrupts known patterns of behavior.

The essays in "Working and Making" conclude that these patterns of behavior, as I have suggested, are intrinsically unstable albeit honored. The instability can be found in the inherent tension between open-endedness and control in architectural design, a tension that plays itself out in many and often contradictory ways: between design (exploratory) and build (practical, exacting);

between design (expansive) and budget (constricting); between technique (infinitely deployable) and material (limiting param-eters); between expressionism (breaking of formal rules) and precision (appreciation of technical rules); between craft (subjec-tive variety) and design (logical premeditation); between vision (economically unconstrained) and marketability (economically constrained).

In the first essay, Kenneth Frampton, in his argument that parametric and digital technology instrumentalize design, throws down the gauntlet regarding what he feels is at stake for craft, authenticity, and responsible authorship. In many ways this essay represents what other authors are up against as they make claims for a more positive and expanded notion of craft and design in architecture.

In this regard, Scott Marble's essay evaluates what craft means today and lays out many of the concerns picked up by authors in this section: the issue of control (or lack thereof) that arises with parametric design; the question of whether techniques/tools or material should be given primacy in fabrication; and the role of the imagination in a technologically sophisticated (read: deterministic) environment. In the digital age, Marble says, no longer can the word *craft* be identified solely with the hand that works physical material. It must also encompass the mind that can command the operations of technology, which can be understood as intellectual "material." He identifies the risk inherently involved in craft but suggests that unlike in the past, where risk lay in the transition from designer to craftsman/builder, today it rests in the capabilities of the human imagination. Mark Goulthorpe and Jamie Carpenter offer more specific, yet contrasting, descriptions of what they privilege as good "craft," with Goulthorpe emphasizing the value of material-neutral techniques provided by parametric design and Carpenter emphasizing the fast-disappearing concern for materiality. Goulthorpe examines the formal potential within a set of given surface-defining parameters, finding that traditional notions of space, time, and movement are radically reconfigured. Carpenter insists that it is just such computer-driven formal concerns that ignore material phenomena and yield zinc as the contemporary wallpaper.

Kolarevic then returns us to the issue of risk, but where Mar-ble equates parametrics—and technology in general—with control and imagination with risk, Kolarevic characterizes risk as an inher-ent attribute of parameterics, based as it is on relationships whose formal outcome cannot be predicted. Likewise, Kolarevic and Marble have comparable but diverging views of efficiency. Marble links efficiency not to the speed with which parametrics spin out variations but with the efficiency of the human imagination; he thus links risk (positively) to efficiency. Kolarevic finds efficiency in the ability of the iterative parametric process to provide alternatives but sees inefficiency in its nonlinear open-endedness; he thus links risk (positively) to inefficiency. The question of risk and efficiency lingers in the essays of Carpenter and Goulthorpe as well. Carpenter is clear that digital technology's ability to preview technical difficulties reduces costly risk in production. Goulthorpe appreciates the transparency—if not exactly the efficiency—of digital processes that makes design, in the collapse between intention and execution, protoimmediate. Kevin Rotheroe, in his essay, then attaches the issue of craft to the idea of value. Acknowledging that craft—be it manual or machinic—costs money, he suggests that the proliferation of computer numerical control (CNC) precision promotes the positive reception of craft in general. In his concentration on notions of craft as human versus technical, his concerns are related to Marble's, although for Marble, the "human" rests in the imagination, not the hand.

In connecting the value, both social and economic, of craft to the cost/value of labor, Rotheroe's essay corresponds with mine, which looks at the issue of design and craft labor through the lens of detail. I argue that the dichotomy between *detail* and *craft* and the historical shift concerning which term is privileged achieves a kind of resolution in current parametric and digital-fabrication practice. At the same time, the nineteenth-century architectural theorist's obsession with the craft laborer reemerges and provides an opportunity to more positively address the status of contemporary makers *and* designers. Coren Sharples then provides a discussion of exactly what this implies for her firm, SHoP Architects. Sharples gives an account of the development of the complex brick panels used in a Houston Street, New York, apartment building, describing the manner in which building information modeling (BIM) allows the architect to function as a leader for the client and as a collaborator with the builder; a dispersion, in other words, of authorship. The impediment to a fully realized reidentification of the architect/author is the culture of the architectural office itself, where the inherent tension between partners ("management") and staff ("workforce") needs to be actively combated and the common stake in design research promoted. While craft does not come into Sharples's picture, the design process is redefined here to encompass organizing design and construction procurement, and its object is less the building (or, in this case, the facade) than the logic of its delivery.

Finally, Kent Larson describes a project, House-n, that takes this notion of design to its logical conclusion. The development of so-called design engines that allow a layperson to efficiently create and purchase his or her own home environment removes, Larson argues, any need for craft; instead, the user-designer sources products. But even the realization that sourcing is only as good as the yet-to-be-designed universal interface leaves craft at the mercy of its traditional enemy: standardization. Larson extends the technological imperatives of digital prototyping to factory assembly and asks if the computational solutions—not unlike Goulthorpe's algorithmic imperatives—can act as design configurators, rapidly displaying and, it is hoped, procuring the desired consumer product.

In "Collaboration," the second section of this book, the contributors explore instabilities that are, again, embedded in long-standing architectural practice but aggravated by digital technology. These tensions pertain to the ambiguities and contradictions inherent in the roles of the players in the building process, particularly with regard to expectation, intention, and execution: the ambiguity between client (laying out intention), architect (laying out own intention versus executing client's), and builder (executing client's intention versus architect's intention); the ambiguity between architect (laying out intention), general contractor (reinterpreting architect's intention), and subcontractor (executing contractor's intention); the ambiguity between primary stakeholders (trying to expedite a project) and expert consultants (indicating that the stakeholders do not fully know how to do that); and the ambiguity between stakeholders (trying to execute a project) and lawyers/contracts (trying to limit liability).

Paolo Tombesi's essay, which opens the section, suggests that architects are obliged—though for the most part have failed—to design a process by which their aesthetic intent can be realized. A successful process would acknowledge the nonlinear movement from intent to execution. In the flexible specialization Tombesi promotes, every aspect of the design-to-build process can be considered an aspect of design production, with designers, fabricators, builders, and programmers all claiming an area of special expertise within the domain of design. Tombesi argues that as the means of modern production move from straight lines to networks, so, too, does the labor of building. John Taylor explores the organization of the network itself as it struggles to accommodate innovation. Diagramming the fact that innovations practiced in one part of the network not only may not produce innovations in others but may actually hinder its proliferation, Taylor implicitly argues for the need to change the traditional interdependencies embedded in the network. In this way, Taylor's assessment of innovation mirrors Tombesi's emphasis on the protocols of nonlinear movements between design and production specialties: it is labor's inability/resistence to organize itself with flexibility and dexterity, not technology, that is an obstacle to a radically changed system of production.

Attorney Howard Ashcraft, who is at the forefront of defining new contract models for innovative delivery models, suggests that the development of information sharing, BIM in particular, is as much a process as it is a technology, and that as a process, it leads to collaboration. Wider adoption of BIM will increase pressure to institutionalize collaboration and move toward integration. Ashcraft argues that although collaboration is traditionally not well supported by our design and construction business, new protocols remove roadblocks that have been our traditional pretext for slow adaptation. Structural engineer Rodd Merchant also argues that advanced technology—interoperability—is not the sine qua non for breaking down siloized, self-protective design to building procedures and that progress lies in resisting existing contractual relationships binding engineers and other consultants to architects. In the design-build model—here demonstrated with an example from a steel construction company—the engineering is subcontracted by the fabricator, and coordination is internalized by the team. The centrality of contractual relationships also guides attorney Chris Noble's examination of intellectual property standards in design. While copyrights are a minor issue when, as he says, little is at stake, "what is 'at stake' can be multiplied exponentially" with the production of digital information that can be leveraged over the life cycle of one and many projects. In this case, contracts and licensing become more important than ever, which highlights the virtually dysfunctional lack of coordination in the current system of contracts. Noble suggests that improved coordination needs to be modeled on extranet contracts, such as those that govern the downloading of software, thus determining control of intellectual property by control of its allocation.

In Phillip Bernstein's "Marketing and Positioning Design," the issue of contracts recedes, but that of authorship, implicit in the question of copyrights, arises full force. Because marketing assumes a degree of standardization—one needs to be able to fix and brand a product—the marketable architectural product tends to leave, as Bernstein points out, individual identity behind. At the same time, positioning in the marketplace requires differentiation from one's competition, and with this, perhaps not authorship but product uniqueness matters greatly. As his examination of four different producers of standardized housing shows, the repeatable unit that is at the center of marketing in this case is not the typical kind, which threatens consumer choice. Instead, what is undermined is architectural ego. And so we return to the issue raised in

"Working and Making": in the context of mass production, mass customization, and digital fabrication, where precisely does design authorship reside, and does it depend on evidence of individual expression? It destabilizes, in any case, what and where we think "design" actually is in the mass-produced/customized object.

In the concluding essay to this section, Bernstein reflects on the central issue of this volume: what is the full potential of new digital protocols and parametric potential? The replacement of the traditional working drawing—put in place to bridge the divide between thinker (architect, intention) and maker (constructor, execution)—with "behaviorally accurate, 3-D digital prototypes of designs" changes not only the nature of design work but the relationship between designers, constructor, subcontractors, and clients. Echoing the essential theme of collaboration allowed and demanded by the integrated delivery approach espoused by Howard Ashcraft, Bernstein suggests that innovation will be driven not by the architect's desire for design control and virtuosity but by the client's desire for profitability and efficiency. He also posits that this desire need not come at the expense of the architect or builder but that it can be dispersed between them. In the sharing of risks and rewards, the controversy over project control gives way, as he says, to *leadership* as players take on authority when their expertise is required. In this, Bernstein echoes Tombesi, who insists that the concept of design be migratory and shared in just this way.

What emerges from this volume is the fact that architecture is poised either to become increasingly irrelevant or to grab this moment of opportunity to reinvent both its protocols and its reach. We hope the profession is up to the task of building (in) the future.

Working and Making

Collaboration

Intention, Craft, and Rationality
Kenneth Frampton

In *The Human Condition* (1958), Hannah Arendt wrote:

> Labor is the activity which corresponds to the biological process of the human body, whose spontaneous growth, metabolism, and eventual decay are bound to the vital necessities produced and fed into the life process by labor.
>
> Work is the activity which corresponds to the unnatural-ness of human existence, which is not embedded in, and whose mortality is not compensated by, the species' ever-recurring life cycle. Work provides an "artificial" world of things, distinctly different from all natural surroundings. Within its borders each individual life is housed, while this world itself is meant to out-last and transcend them all. The human condition of work is worldliness.[1]

The other keyword implicitly connected to the Arendtian distinction between *labor* and *work* is the term *craft*. The presence or absence of craftsmanship as a practice is evidently linked to the alienation experienced to a greater or lesser degree in the division of labor that attends all forms of production. The fulfillment through crafts-manship of the *homo faber* is that which fundamentally saves him from the fate of *animal laborans*. As Arendt put it:

> If the *animal laborans* needs the help of *homo faber* to ease his labour and remove his pain, and if mortals need his help to erect a home on earth, acting and speaking men need the help of *homo faber* in his highest capacity, that is, the help of the artist, of poets and historiographers, of monument-builders or writers, because without them the only product of their activity, the story they enact and tell, would not survive at all. In order to be what the world is always meant to be, a home for men during their life on earth, the human artifice must be a place fit for action and speech, for activities not entirely useless for the necessities of life but of an entirely different nature from the manifold activities of fabrication by which the world itself and all things in it are produced.[2]

For Arendt, the *homo faber* was at once the builder of the human cosmos that stands in opposition to the chaos of nature and the inventor and maker of the instruments with which the world is built. If the first aspect addresses the "what" of representation and

1 Hannah Arendt, *The Human Condition* (Chicago: University of Chicago Press, 1958), 7.

2 Arendt, *Human Condition*, 173–74.

creation of a human world, the second concerns itself with the
"how" of process, utility, and fabrication.

Perhaps no architect has thought more synthetically
about this symbiotic relationship between the what and the how
than B. Scott Francisco. In his "Usable Space: Culture vs. Technology in Pursuit of Design," he defined the complex relationship
obtaining between intentionality, tradition, craft, and design in
the following way:

> Unlike in design (where intentions are manifest in the gap
> *between* planning and making) in tradition they are located in
> the *contact* between "a way of making" and the origin of the
> activity that is rooted in communal identity…In tradition, inten-
> tionality is generally *concealed* by an appeal to "how something
> *was*, and therefore *should be*, done." Design, on the other hand,
> celebrates itself as a *rupture with context*, making a virtue of
> individual choice in the face of any *status quo*…
>
> Design, in this sense, is a fundamentally modern concept,
> effectively relying on *specification* for realization, while at the
> same time, giving tremendous agency to subjectivity.[3]

He continued:

> Enter *parametric* design in architecture [in which] digital design
> tools are used to establish particular relationships between
> predetermined elements so that a change in a variable will
> *automatically* result in a "chain reaction" between elements that
> have been programmed to react in a particular way…This tech-
> nique can be applied to optimizing anything, traffic lights, flight
> paths, manufacturing floors and potentially even the design of
> whole new cities. Parametrics becomes a system for replacing
> the "repetitive tasks" of subjective thought (along with all of
> their imbedded intention and indeterminable vagaries) with the
> computer's programmatic logic.[4]

Hence, Francisco went on to note, computer programs recently
developed by the Dutch firm MVRDV, with seductive titles like *City-
maker*, *Regionmaker*, *Climatizer*, and even *Idealizer*, are designed
to yield optimized subsets of what we might call authorless results.

The process and limitations of parametric digital design
prompt us to pass from the rather abstract issue of intentionality
to the problem of rationality as an end in itself, which leads us to

3   B. Scott Francisco, "Usable Space: Culture vs. Technology in Pursuit of   Design" (master's thesis, Massachusetts Institute of Technology, 2005), 21, 23.   4   Francisco, "Usable Space," 81, 83.

question the a priori variables obtaining in any particular chain of
rational thought; that is to say, to question which rationalization we
have in mind, for which subject, and to what end.

In his lecture entitled "Rationalism and Man," Alvar Aalto
pointed out that *rationalism* is a viable term in architecture only if it
takes in psychological and not merely technological determinants:

> Thus we might say that one way to produce a more humane
> built environment is to extend our definition of rationalism...
> Even if a more precise analysis were to lead to the conclusion
> that some emotional concept is the sum of elements that are
> physically or otherwise measurable, we would still soon find our-
> selves outside the realm of physics. A whole series of questions
> that can be asked of virtually every object, but have hitherto
> been very seldom considered, surely relates to another science
> altogether, psychology. As soon as we include psychological
> requirements or, rather, as soon as we are able to include them,
> we will have extended the rationalist working method enough to
> make it easier to prevent inhuman results.[5]

Aalto reminded us that our mode of reasoning is only apposite
if we bear in mind, from the beginning, the relationship between
means and ends and so avoid the aporia in which means determine ends. Architecture by definition aspires to a state of cultural
synthesis and so cannot be made totally consistent in terms of
criteria whose sole aim is to optimize production as an end in itself,
since at its best, building culture incorporates values that tran-
scend our current proclivity for maximizing the production/con-
sumption cycle in every facet of life. At the same time, the material
and operative transformations taking place in the building industry
cannot be ignored by the profession, if for no other reason than
that many of these innovations are coming from the profession
itself. It is in this light that we are once more being subjected to the
invidious comparison between our backward building industry and
the sophisticated techniques of the technology currently employed
in the Taylorized production of automobiles and aircraft.

One notes that the market for cars and planes is structurally
different from that in the field of built form, where the product is
not a freestanding object reducible to the status of a commodity.
At the same time, the dematerialization of building that has taken
place in the last half century has totally transformed the distribution of costs involved in the realization of a structure. Although the

5 Alvar Aalto, "Rationalism and Man,"
in *Alvar Aalto in His Own Words*, ed.
Göran Schildt (Rizzoli, 1998), 90–91.

cost of placing a structure in the ground has remained constant across a long period of time, the largest segment in any building budget today is devoted to the provision of electrical and mechanical services, with the result that the proportion spent on the enclosure has dropped from around 80 percent at the beginning of the twentieth century to approximately 20 percent today. This largely accounts for the dematerialization of built form that we witness in the universal application of the curtain wall throughout the developed world, irrespective of whether it is of glass, metal, or some other relatively lightweight material.

One cannot avoid remarking on the techno-utopic language that has accompanied the emergence of digital design and construction, particularly with respect to its seemingly limitless potential to realize spaces and forms hitherto unimagined. While this productive potential is surely realizable and even, to a degree, unavoidable in a great deal of contemporary building production, it is as yet only in its infancy as far as its future application is concerned. In this regard, architects and educators need to reassess the limits of the profession within the worldwide panorama of contemporary production. With or without the advantages of parametric design, the hard fact remains that some 90 percent of the annual built production in the United States still takes place without the intervention of any architect whatsoever—a statistic that should give us pause as we proclaim our newfound technological capacity. The rhetoric the profession employs borders on techno-idolatry, recalling the scientific discourse of Buckminster Fuller and Marshall McLuhan and coloring the present moment in architecture, in which demand for spectacular, mediatic images eclipses critical reflection.

A computer numerical control (CNC) off-site fabricator is of necessity indifferent to the ultimate destiny of the parts he or she is producing: automobile body one day, building curtain wall the next. Despite CNC's basis in the already well-established practice of partial off-site fabrication, there is surely a considerable measure of technological boosterism, riding on the rhetoric of a globalized "knowledge-based economy" in which the professional either sinks or swims according to his or her digital capacity.

Surprising as it may seem, this technological euphoria is not shared by most structural and environmental engineers, who are both more discriminate and more secure with regard to their professional role within the building industry. In the "Versioning" issue of *Architectural Design*, this much is boldly commented on by Peter Westbury of Buro Happold when he reminds his colleagues of the long-standing, rather obvious interface between architecture and engineering, which might be represented as two interlocking, overlapping circles. This concept of collaborative practice is hardly new, since it was already elaborated on by Le Corbusier's dialogical scheme of 1948, in which he depicted the interplay between *l'homme spirituel* and *l'homme economique*, the opposing identities of architect and engineer, as they make their respective contributions according to their respective métiers.

This mediatory model of symbiotic practice is compromised totally by that not uncommon contemporary challenge confronting the engineer when he or she has to make a crumpled piece of paper or its equivalent stand up. Of this intrinsic irrationality West-bury is only too critical:

> How can you expect an engineering solution…to be anything other than dumb if we impose external influences on form that are completely abstracted from any technology? Let's not forget where Modernism and the machine age came from, it came from technology…I don't mind coming up with a dumb solution that goes between two skins of sculpture designed by a screwed-up piece of paper, but it is not really where I get my kicks.[6]

This syndrome accompanies the irrational and often culturally neg-ative conjunction between smart technology and gratuitousness of self-indulgent form, particularly when the latter is conceived as sculpture writ large, as one more freestanding aesthetic object that however sophisticated is totally indifferent to the topographic context in which it is situated.

A corollary to this is the unavoidable contemporary emphasis on cladding—preferably synthetic and fabricated off-site and assembled dry. This formula is optimized to the exclusion of all other considerations, save for the authorless morphed blob designed to produce an arresting, spectacular image—seen as the touchstone of mediative success in a world saturated with imagery competing for attention. Thus we are confronted not only with a fetishistic emphasis on the membrane as an end in itself but also with the problematic displacement of the "what" by the "how."

Today, however, we cannot dispose of the "what" quite so lightly, particularly in view of the growing incapacity of the architectural profession to limit itself to the generation of an appropriate space-form capable of responding to the site, to the climate, to the available materials, and above all to the institutional parameters of the building program—exactly those factors that are

6   Paul Westbury, "The Buro Happold Tapes," *Architectural Design* 72, no. 5 (September–October 2002): 75–77.

the embodied values of the situation, as much political as spiritual in their intentionality. The mediation of such values through architecture is a task that does not reside within the province of the engineer, nor is it exclusively within that of the architect. Instead it lies at the interface between them, with the architect—a "specialist in non-specialization," to quote Álvaro Siza's ironic phrase—being the one figure who has to arrive at an appropriate a priori point of departure for the team, the valid space-form/place-form. Today, given the fact that in the so-called developed world buildings consume some 40 percent of our total energy consumption, there is perhaps no more crucial specialist member of this team than the environmental engineer, who is increasingly becoming indispensable as a consultant in the ultimate refinement of architectural form. One should also note the crucial role to be played by the landscape architect, without whom no building may be adequately grounded today, notwithstanding all the other technical specialists who are essential to the makeup of a comprehensive design team for a building of any size.

When it comes to the position of the architect as exemplifying the *homo faber* through his leadership of the team, perhaps no other architect has so pertinently defended the idea of craft as Renzo Piano, who is inclined to see craft as the common unifying principle in the elaboration of teamwork. It is surely significant that Piano elected to practice under the name of Renzo Piano Building Workshops:

> An architect must be a craftsman. Of course any tools will do. These days the tools might include a computer, an experimental model and mathematics. However, it is still craftsmanship—the work of someone who does not separate the work of the mind from the work of the hand. It involves a circular process that draws you from an idea to a drawing, from a drawing to an experiment, and from a construction back to an idea again. For me this cycle is fundamental to creative work. Unfortunately many have come to accept each of these steps as independent…Teamwork is essential if creative projects are to come about. Teamwork requires an ability to listen and engage in a dialogue.[7]

Piano's practice also seeks to expand the notion of craftsmanship to embrace the idea of a continual creative exchange between manual and intellectual work: an exchange that would implicitly

7   "Renzo Piano Building Workshop: In Search of Balance," *Process Architecture* (Tokyo), 100 (1992): 12, 14.

renounce the split between art and science through the untrans-
latable Greek term *techne*, which according to Martin Heidegger
means a mode of knowing that is inseparable from creativity. Piano
continued the image of the circle when writing about research:

> You test what you have found. If it does not work you start again.
> You formulate another hypothesis and go back over what you
> have done and so on. In the process, you narrow the circle, like
> a hawk closing in on its prey. Note that circularity in this sense,
> it is not just methodology, and still less a procedure. It is to use
> high-sounding words a theory of knowledge.[8]

Through such a procedure, design flows into research and vice
versa, while building art (the German term *Baukunst*) may take
precedence over the monumental connotations of architecture
qua architecture in a classical sense. Along with this goes a renun-
ciation of any kind of self-conscious signature that is identifiable
as a style or a brand. Replacing it is an unspoken acceptance
that not every project is capable of being brought to the same
level of resolution.

These concerns, combined with a profound respect for
craft, serve to separate the ethos of the Piano workshop from the
parametrical formalist obsessions that currently prevail in elite
architecture schools on both sides of the Atlantic. As is common
knowledge, the studios of these schools indulge in aestheticized
morphing exercises that, while they are brilliantly contrived and
graphically seductive, are invariably unspecific as to the substance
of the project, not only in terms of site, materials, structure, and
environmental performance, but also with regard to the basic
raison d'etre underlying the supposed function or programmatic
address of the work in hand. With this phenomenon we are confronted with the paradox of Beaux Arts architecture in neo-avant-
gardist dress. This syndrome could hardly be farther removed from
the relative realism of high tech architecture.

Globalized high tech architecture is no panacea, however,
because despite the phenomenon of globalization, building cul-
tures remain very different as one passes from one country to the
next, one region to the next, or one climate to the next, and, most
certainly, one fabricator to the next. What is possible to achieve in
one locale at a particular price cannot necessarily be reproduced
at the same level of precision in another situation for the same
price or, for that matter, by another fabricator in the same locale.

8 Renzo Piano, *Renzo Piano:
Logbook* (New York: Monacelli Press,
1997), 18.

This explains high-end structures such as Norman Foster's canonical Hong Kong and Shanghai Bank (1986), which was assembled from components prefabricated in many different countries and transported to the job by air—for example, tubular steel from the UK and prefabricated toilet facilities from Japan.

The realization of this masterwork recalls the time-honored rivalry between architect and builder, not to mention all the attendant players who jockey for position within the everyday work of realizing a building: the engineers, fabricators, contractors, and construction managers, as well as the multitude of sundry technical consultants. There was a time, a century or more ago, when the newly formed architectural profession, backed by the commissioning power of the state, was able to exert its authority over the then rather limited know-how of the building industry. This has changed over the last forty years, in part because the profession of architecture has been deregulated, the aim being the transformation of the liberal professions into separate sectors of a comprehensive service industry driven by the market.

One might note in passing, as others have done at different times, the power accruing to the architect when he or she is totally integrated with a building enterprise's capacity to build. This was the case with Auguste Perret's practice in the first half of the twentieth century, and something similar is obtained, at a vastly increased scale, in the large Japanese contracting firms such as Takenaka, Taisai, and Obayashi, which maintain large in-house teams of architects and engineers who not only design and detail the entire output of their respective companies but also in effect redraw or redesign any project coming to the firm from independent architects.

But this ability to cross over the design versus build divide is the exception, as is the opportunity to celebrate the actual building. Joshua Prince-Ramus touches on this unreal split between the media cult of the individual star and the anonymity of divided labor that realizes the work:

The split of Architects into Project Architects and Project Managers is a direct consequence of our profession's cowardice… We hijacked authorship, diverting it from process (the synthesis of creation and execution) to creation alone. We banished Project Managers to the realm of *expertise*, then derided them for succumbing to power and wealth. If Architects can reprioritize authorship of processes over authorship of things, we can reassemble Project Architects and Project Managers back into Architects. We will regain liability, but re-harvest control. And we will be able to happily navigate from concept generation, through politics, value-engineering and procurement strategies, to punch lists and opening parties. We will harbor less self-pity, make more money and construct better architecture.[9]

His accompanying challenge to both the concept of singular authorship and the avoidance of risk (as he puts it, losing control) brings us to an intractable issue: how should the architects of the future be educated or, more urgently, how should our present system of professional training be modified to benefit tomorrow's architects?

   This question is, in and of itself, full of risk, and the academic establishment is showing few signs of confronting this issue head-on, despite the presence of a totally new breed of young architects-academics capable of working at both an intellectual and a manual-cum-technical level. And it would be hard to imagine anything more pedagogically counterproductive than perpetuating the largely unacknowledged fiction that it is possible to cultivate through education the romantic notion of a perennial avant-garde, along with the equally absurd idea of a school for geniuses. Instead we should be equipping the younger generation with a deeper and more sober idea of the limits of the modern project in both a political and technical sense. At the same time, we should be encouraging an examination of an equally pernicious contemporary, Candide-like myth regarding the unavoidable market benefits of globalization in combination with the fictitious worldwide triumph of liberal democracy.

9   Joshua Prince-Ramus, "OMANY: Seattle Central Library, Seattle, USA, 2004," *A + U: Architecture and Urbanism* (May 2006): 98.

Imagining Risk
Scott Marble

If *craft* is defined as a skill developed over time and in direct relationship to making and to working with materials, architects have
long been disconnected from this skill, relying instead on builders
and fabricators to actually carry out their designs. Architects work
with abstract processes of representation that lead to abstract
processes of making. This is a challenging context within which to
position craft, in any conventional definition of the term. For craft
to function as a useful concept today, especially in the context
of digital design and production, it might best be rethought as a
process of mediating not only between tools and the objects that
are produced but also between design as a process of imagination
and production as a process of technique.

In fact, craft has always been mediated through a relationship between humans and technology. From primitive hand tools to
industrialized machines, the quality of craft in an object has been
measured by the trace of human input. Today, with the wide range
of digital technology being used to increase the efficiencies of
human labor (or bypass it altogether), it is useful once again to take
measure: to look critically at how digital mediation is restructuring
design and production and, consequently, redefining craft.

Digital processes in architecture have generally followed
one of three directions that are only now beginning to come
together into a coherent system of architectural production. The
first was the replacement of geometry with a new formal logic
based on mathematics, where scripts or codes generated topological relationships that resulted in complex form. The second
direction was a drive toward organizational complexity, where vast
amounts of information about a building could be input, linked, and
managed. And the third was the development of digital fabrication,
where craft is often considered to have gained a new life through
the direct linking of architects to the tools that make their designs.
Techniques of dimensional or geometric representation, formerly
part of an abstract process of drawing, have evolved into an integrated system of design information embedded in production and
assembly processes. As architect and theorist Stan Allen notes
in his article "Artificial Ecologies," the practice of architecture
has always been in the paradoxical position of being invested in
the production of real, concrete matter yet working with tools of
abstract representation (drawings, models, computer simulations,
and so forth). He goes on to suggest that today even construction
has come to rely on tools of abstraction as computer technology is
increasingly used during the production of buildings.[1]

1 Stan Allen, "Artificial Ecologies," in
Reading MVRDV, ed. Véronique Patteeuw
(Rotterdam: NAi, 2003), 82–87.

Although still mediated through forms of abstract representation, computer numerical control (CNC) systems put the process
of design closer to the production of buildings, merging production
and design into a common language of digital information. The
significance of this should not be underestimated, as this seemingly benign shift in how we communicate carries the potential not
only to reconnect to craft but also to completely restructure the
organization and hierarchy of the design and building industry. This
has been apparent at least since the first integrated design and
fabrication software was tested in design offices in the early 1990s,
with Frank Gehry's Fish Pavilion for the 1992 Olympics in Barcelona
standing as a benchmark.

Craft in architecture is closely tied to detail, which is also
being redefined with digital technology. Architectural detail, an
architect's means of introducing craft into buildings, is largely a
product of the relationship of design to industry. If the modernist's
detail was based on negotiating tolerances between premanufac-
tured components that were then assembled, today's details are
based on the management and organization of information, where
tolerances and even assembly procedures can be numerically
controlled and parametrically integrated during design. Although
these new methods of production do not put architects in the
field literally working with their hands, it does reconnect them
with making—through information and through a more symbiotic
relationship between human intelligence and machine intelligence.
Craft does not disappear but rather expands to include not only
actual making but design processes. The resistance of material, so
much a part of traditional craft, can be part of a knowledge base
developed through feedback, both real and simulated, that puts
this information in the hands of designers who in turn work with it.

The separation between design and production propagated
by industrialized mass production was largely due to a lack of
mediation, that is, a lack of any effective connection between
designers and factory workers. And although this spurred on
several attempts to appropriate industrialized processes for use in
innovative design (for example, by the Deutscher Werkbund, the
Bauhaus, and the Case Study House Program), these were atypi-
cal and short-lived exercises, because industry and manufacturing
remained primarily driven by purely economic imperatives. In the
meantime, architecture drifted toward design that defined itself
as distinct from the goals of industry. It is this lack of mediation
between design and production that is being reformulated with
integrated digital design and fabrication processes: drawings and
models are no longer used to represent design "intent"; rather, they

are used to communicate precise information on how to fabricate and with which material.

As the industrialized production of objects of all scales became ubiquitous in the middle of the twentieth century, David Pye positioned craft in direct opposition to this trend, in an effort to salvage what he saw as an invaluable variability associated with human input. He identified craft with the "workmanship of risk"— where the result of working with a material is "not predetermined, but depends on the judgment, dexterity and care" of the maker. "(T)he quality of the result is continually at risk during the process of making," but the payoff is a singular object that serves the broader cultural purpose of sustaining diversity and variation.[2] By contrast, he associated the "workmanship of certainty" with industrialization, and in particular, with mass production and automation, where the refinement of the process assures a predetermined result. For Pye, clearly something was lost in the uniformity and repetition of mass production if carried too far, and something about the risk of craftsmanship was worth preserving.

Although Pye was writing at a time when industrialized processes had already significantly changed the landscape of design, it seems prudent to reevaluate the continuing trend toward certainty today, which is driving the increased use of performance-based design software by architects. In the forty-plus years since the publication of Pye's book, certainty has become nothing short of an economic and social mandate as techniques of simulation combined with exponentially growing bodies of knowledge allow us to anticipate or even predict outcomes. Whereas Pye was referring primarily to manufacturing, the pursuit of certainty and predictability has now come to have a significant impact on the process of design, since modeling, simulation, and optimization software can predict virtually any physical or environmental behavior of materials, systems, and buildings. The more ambitious forms of simulation even attempt to calculate the behavior of people, as in the determination of egress scenarios in crowd-control and life-safety crisis situations.

Risk, on the other hand, is to be avoided at all costs. We want performance. We want to know what we are getting— structurally, aesthetically, financially, even emotionally. Certainty in the form of mass production has, to a large extent, run its course, and the variation associated with risk, which Pye found significant as a kind of "authentic" variation produced by the human hand, has ironically become automated in the form of mass customization—

2 David Pye, *The Nature and Art of Workmanship* (London: Cambridge University Press, 1968), 2.

a kind of "engineered" variation. No part is the same, each product is original; so everyone can, through product purchase, be an individual. In a strange twist, the variation and diversity Pye associated with cultural progress has become endless variation and, in the process, ceased to produce difference. Computation has exaggerated the broad social and cultural tendency toward knowledge leading to predetermined outcomes (certainty), and despite the association of ideas such as mass customization, variation, and difference with current digital processes, what we are experiencing is arguably a continuation and acceleration of a modernist obsession with control, optimization, and efficiency through machine processes. Have digital technologies taken certainty to an extreme, leading to a new, high-resolution technical determinism that has eliminated risk? If not, what are the limits of certainty, and where can these be located today in the context of digital technologies?

The questions around the relationship between human input and technological determinism that arose with industrialization reemerge with digital technology. Most significantly, the industrialized machine that displaced the physical labor of the human body is now being developed as an intelligent machine that displaces the labor of the human mind. Risk is still associated with human input but shifts from the hand (with industrialization) to the mind (with computation). In an increasingly digital working environment driven by an interest in and reliance on performance, scripting, and other deterministic design and production processes, the crucial issue becomes when to utilize numeric processing and when to utilize human imagination.

CNC processing systems have their origins, as one might expect, in the military's effort to assure uniformity and control in the manufacturing of weapons. Their concerns revolved around eliminating any error or friction in the command chain, which consequently meant the elimination of human intervention. As the philosopher of modern science Manual DeLanda has noted, the dream of moving toward a totally computer-controlled factory was one way of assuring this control, even though it was by no means the most efficient one. "Rival technologies, coupling human skills with the power of the computer in different ways, existed but were displaced by NC—the alternative human-machine interfaces did not allow the degree of command and control needed in a logistic system."[3] This occurred, however, with certain long-term implications, as these production processes shifted to the civilian sector.

3 Manuel DeLanda, *War in the Age of Intelligent Machines* (New York: Zone Books, 1991), 33.

Control was maintained but at the cost of efficiency and innovation. How can we learn from the marginalization of human input associated with industrialization and the subsequent attempt to completely eliminate human input through development of the early numerical control systems—systems that are the foundation of our digital technology today? It would seem that, as opposed to an either/or relationship, a back-and-forth play between humans and machines (risk and certainty) has become increasingly important.

Among the most challenging aspects of the development of intelligent machines has been the transfer of knowledge from humans to computers. This pursuit has forced human intelligence to be defined to a degree of quantitative precision such that it can be written and therefore transferred through computer code. Artificial intelligence and cognitive science have evolved together as reciprocal models in this process, each aiding the development of the other while uncovering irreconcilable yet useful differences that are important to acknowledge. The transfer of factual knowledge resulting in highly specific expert systems is relatively straightforward and offers very little toward the understanding of human intelligence. On the other hand, heuristic knowledge—experiential intelligence acquired over years of work; the art of good, informed guessing—is not hard and fast and relies on various forms of inference systems in order to be written in code. This process begins to probe the more complex aspects of human intelligence, testing the limits of artificially mapping the mind.

The most difficult, if not impossible, mental process to quantify and write in code is the contextualization of information—how to simultaneously process an abundance of information and decipher what is relevant and what is not in a given situation—something that is arguably fundamental to design. This is the mental and, by extension, physical agility that Pye was referring to when he distinguished between the variability and risk of human input and the repetition and certainty of the machine.

But risk has a resiliency that is essential to cultural and technological progress—it is where innovation occurs. Certainty, in the form of technical precision, is always short lived, always overcome by cultural interpretation. So while current digital technology delivers increasing amounts of certainty, it is the risk associated with interpreting and imagining alternative outcomes that needs to be maintained to give craft a new role in mediating between humans and technology.

Parametric Profligacy, Radical Economy
Mark Goulthorpe

**So you've embodied movement;
so now can I dance my house?
—Heidi Gilpin**

Heidi Gilpin, ex-dramaturge of the Frankfurt Ballet, had specified "embodied movement" as an impetus for the design of her summer house on Grand Isle, that forlorn sandbar sheltering the New Orleans estuary, whose own topography is continually shifting through deposition and erosion. Set within the recurrently scarred posthurricane landscape, the house was intended as a temporary retreat for the academic to complete a book on trauma, a concept she interrogates to account for contemporary works that engender cultural affect as if through the very inassimilability of their generative process(es): where the event is "missed" in the very intensity of its occurrence.

   Her other prerequisite for the Hi-D Haus, as it was named, was that the house "make time," which, given the intense focus on absented presence that is at issue in accounts of trauma, was taken to mean something other than that it provide a robotic housekeeper! Indeed, dECOi—my architectural firm—took it as a plea (given the latency implicit in her belabored book) for the capture of operational lubricity, for an effortless instantiation of form/function articulacy.

   Many of the resulting Massachusetts Institute of Technology (MIT) studio designs deployed open-ended digital generative processes, enigmatic in their post-hand-eye formal complexity and often eerily beautiful in their second-order geometric logic. Yet it was not the formal sophistication of such trappings of the dynamic

Jimmy Shen, Hi-D Haus,
House design for Heidi
Gilpin, Grand Isle
Massachusetts Institute
of Technology studio
project, 2008

aspects of the (generative) environment that caught Gilpin's attention, but a sketch-design tool as it was demonstrated live by a design student (Jimmy Shen) and a computation PhD (Kaustuv De Biswas). This was an applet they had developed using "processing" (a force-particle computational protocol) to permit sophisticated yet gestural 3-D sketching that could be materially instantiated at any given moment. Their architectural design was not so much a formal proposition as it was a processural one, no longer an architecture but the possibility of an architecture, a form-force potency.

The speed and direction of the drawing gesture released particles in space, a kind of 3-D calligraphy. Yet the particles were dynamically linked together within the processing environment by unseen elastic force lines that pulled them into relation with the adjacent particles, blurring into soft equilibrium. This seemed akin to the ink-paper absorption that a calligrapher intuits before the decisive brushstroke, requiring a similar preparatory intuition; but here the mental space of the canvas collapsed into depth, nuanced by a hyperbolic expansion of computational proclivity that recalibrated the form-force as if convulsively.[1] The gesture produced fluid lines of blurring material density—Picasso's virtual and time delayed *Bull* becoming actual infomaterial.

Yet here the space-time lines were latent in their momentary settling-into-equilibrium, the forces variable and subject to changing laws, even able to be swept into languid sheets of multistring suspension. Indeed, any elastic line of particles could be subjected to decay, such that on being released they would begin to retract (or expand), as if independent temporal progeny,

Jimmy Shen and Kaustuv De Biswas, 3-D calligraphy particles produced project, Massachusetts Institute of Technology studio project, 2008

1 The Springy Thingy applet, an elastic, 3-D sketch-design tool, was developed by Kaustuv De Biswas and Jimmy Shen, who at the time were students at MIT. The speed of the mouse affected the depth-into-plane of the particles, and the force of the springs streamlined them into locally balanced equilibrium, creating elegant lines in 3-D space.

creating populated string particles/surfaces as families of force-time adjacency.[2]

The students "drew" the house in real time using a "wand," instinct and complex calculus merging as spatial/material densities, the particles self-organizing according to both internal force and external *influence* (floor particles coagulating due to orientation, walls "breathing" open and orienting directionally, and so forth).[3] The resulting shell forms, traces of a proprio-receptive instinct left hanging in space as an active mathematical residue, were quite haunting: forms of architectural calligraphy nuanced in time by an impossibly complex restraint.[4] Implicit within such elegant forms was law and the capacity to regulate the distribution of particles according to structural or environmental agency (a heliotropic or catenary impulsion, for instance) or even variation of material property. The results were simply 3-D printed, emphasizing the material veracity of the process, a sketch-to-form instantaneity, a radical trapping of time.

The spontaneous inhalation, "So you've embodied movement," gave testimony to the formal sophistication of this work, uttered as it was by a refined balletic mind intuitively grasping in an instant the potential for exquisite restraint that such a system offered. But it was the immediate slippage into the exhalation, "so now can I dance my house?" that gave pause to the architectural formalists. This was not formalism, after all, but form-ism, formativ-ism, inner law inflected by intuition, an *implicit* expertise. All this was not lost on the client, since she was a colleague of Bill Forsythe, her colleague and the choreographer of the Frankfurt Ballet, who has radicalized classical dance—not just formally through the parametric-rule sets he deploys (which give exquisite new formal derivatives) but by his allowance of equal status to nonclassically trained dancers, "heart" replacing head or line, as he puts it.[5] The labor force, as it were, is no longer *expert*, except in its aptitude for rule-based generative profligacy. This radicalization of the idea of role was the tacit trace left hanging around the implacable stealth of the 3-D print machine, an intuitive leap from corps de ballet to Z Corp printing.

This may seem a curiously arabesque introduction to the topic of labor, yet I think it epitomizes the latency implicit in

2   Here lines are reproduced and released temporally, giving expanding or contracting series of proximate 3-D lines born of inner law (force).

3   A device used to register 3-D movement as a controlling input, designed and built by John Rothenberg, who at the time was a master's of architecture student at MIT.

4   See Gaston Bachelard's discussion of the formative logic of nests and shells in *The Poetics of Space*, (trans. Maria Jolas, (1964; repr. Boston: Beacon Press, 1994). He asserts that the fundamental quality of both shells and nests is that they are born of a complex inner logic that is left as material trace, not by an external geometric description.

5   The author has written elsewhere about the implications for architecture of the creative experiments of Bill Forsythe's startling revision of balletic protocol. See, for example, "Cut Idea," in Mark Goulthorpe, *The Possibility of (an) Architecture: Collected Essays by Mark Goulthorpe, dECOi Architects* (New York: Routledge, 2008).

digital design technology. I use these terms carefully: *technology* seemingly the mental aptitudes engendered, or impelled, by new technique; and *latency* the impulsion to give such formative logic expression (frequently repressed, if we are to acknowledge the psychoanalytic import of the term).[6] Digital techniques implicitly subtend powerful calculating processes, allowing complex relationships to be made explicit across a range of iterations: this is de facto what they can "do," despite our predilection for using them in ways more akin to familiar techniques. As we adjust mentally to accept this capacity to render explicit the relationships that were hitherto only (for architects) "intuitively" implicit, so we will increasingly come to explore this latent capacity, particularly in areas such as architectural design that clearly require the mastery of complex parametric relationships. We will deploy such logics for the formal sophistication they offer, evidently—a Forsythe-and-after cultural intensity; but we will also use them for their efficiency, their sketch-to-form effortlessness.

This suggests an impact on architectural labor (cultural birthing) as to the labor of architecture (recalibration of work). Is it so radical to suggest that generative intensity—formal, material, technical—and fabrication efficiency might fold together through the agency of digital systems? Even architect Ali Rahim, who was present at the studio review, was impressed by the deep elegance that was proffered: elegance in giving sophisticated agency to intuitive design desire, as much as in the continued expectation that architects produce exemplary singular iterations using such processes. "My utopia," said Norman O'Brown, the pop psychologist, "is an environment that works so well that we can run wild in it."[7] He goes on to suggest that the governance of people will be replaced by "the *administration of things*," which he holds out as a bizarre culmination of the social theory of Karl Marx and Friedrich Engels.

The applet devised for the Hi-D Haus was called Springy Thingy (a name dECOi liked for its antielitist tone), and it has spawned Birdy Wirdy (characterized by vectors rather than particles) and Dust Bunny (or point clouds).[8] The ancestor of these current animate agencies was the Voronoi Bunny applet,

6   For more on *technology* and *cutting*, see "Autoplastic to Alloplastic," in Goulthorpe, *Possibility of (an) Architecture.* There and elsewhere, the author tries to articulate the impulsion that occurs when any new technical process infects creative imagination. Clearly, a period of adaptation occurs before a full understanding, when mental aptitude gropes to attain mastery of the new technique. The desire to express such

changed logic is obviously at issue as we negotiate the transition from mechanical to digital paradigms.

7   Norman O. Brown, "From Politics to MetaPolitics" (Frederic William Atherton lecture, Harvard University, 20 March, 1967). Subsequently published in handwritten form in *Caterpillar* 1 (Fall 1967)

8   Birdy Wirdy is a version of Springy Thingy that substitutes vectors for particles in the same processing-based applet. Birdy Wirdy was also developed by Kaustuv De Biswas.

Dust Bunny is an alternative point-cloud-formative applet devised by John Snavely, a master's of architecture candidate at MIT. Matter is gathered into solid form either by advancing solids through a which was developed as part of the formative logic of the Sin-thome Sculpture, an interdisciplinary design and development workshop cohosted at MIT by the computer science and architecture departments.[9]

The concept of the sinthome was developed by psychoana-lyst Jacques Lacan in his *Seminar 23*, which concerns itself with artistic volition in general but looks specifically at the autopoetic writing of author James Joyce.[10] Lacan invoked the topological figure of the Borromean knot as a model of psychic normalcy, the three interlocked rings representing the Real, the Imaginary, and the Symbolic, each overlapping to create regions of desire and motivation. In Joyce's case, Lacan contended, the three rings had become uncoupled, and Joyce's artistic drive effectively created a fourth ring, a sinthome (symptom) that served to rebind his identity and psyche. This took the form of an interlacing band weaving between the loosely coupled three-ring imbroglio, itself an inherently unstable tripling. Given the essentially mechanical, rule-based nature of Joyce's macaronic writing, at issue was the contested relationship between "mechanical" and "natural" aspects of subjectivity, with Lacan following through on Freud's *Fort/Da* observation that the repetitive automata-like actions of the child are evidently self-constituting and formative.[11] Such an analy-sis, attempting as it does to locate the subjective motivation of Joyce (the epitome of elitist Western academic culturalism) within a man-machine symbiosis, seems prescient within an emerging, now-digital creative paradigm.

Lacan had chosen the sinthome as a second-order geomet-ric figure, elusive to a mind attuned to first-order geometric forms: it demanded a stretch of imagination, or hours of concentrated sketching on the blackboard before his seminars, to capture it. Clearly the sinthome is not a figure as much as a relational condition, an iterable topological state. Yet with parametric digital tools, the MIT workshop was able to model the Borromean knot parametrically and then generate an infinite number of sinthomic variants explicitly, the sheath of the sinthome distorting quite

field of suspended particles to create zones of density or by planting attractor points that coagulate particles in space. Again, force is the formative logic, with elastic adjacency altered differentially in zones.

9 The Voronoi Bunny applet was an algorithmic applet that looks for planar arrangements of Voronoi tiles on any given complex-curved surface. The famous cartoon rabbit form employed by computer scientists to test new software, particularly in 3-D rendering applications, was used to

emphasize the breaching of elitist design regimen as such processes become readily available to a nonspecialist audience.

The workshop at MIT was devised to interrogate the emerging protocols of digital creative processes; specifically, attempting multiprocess—algorithmic, programmatic, parametric—logics. Yet such pressing toward an extreme digital protocol was accompanied by reflection on Jacques Lacan's seminal analysis of James Joyce's creative drive, in particular related to the autopoetic and "mechanical" aspects of his

generative process. At issue was creative subjectivity within automated mechanical and digital generative processes.

10 Jacques Lacan, "James Joyce: Le symptôme," in *Autres écrits*. (Paris: Seuil, 2001)

11 See Sigmund Freud's case study of the game fort/da that his grandson played, hid-ing and finding a cotton-reel that the child took as a symbol for the mother.

Jimmy Shen with Mark
Goulthorpe, Sinthome
form, 2008

>
Mark Goulthorpe,
Sinthome Paramorph,
Bankside Paramorph,
2008

<
Mark Goulthorpe,
algorithmic Voronoi
diagram, 2008

radically with small inflections of the controlling rings. Indeed, what became most compelling, as we automated the model to spew thousands of sinthome forms each night, was the extent to which, even with such explicit control, the forms wildly exceeded our imagination through some second-order agency that we struggled to assimilate intellectually. We found ourselves utterly absorbed in adapting alloplastically to the 3=4 profligate breach of determinism, where a strict rule set entices imagination through its precise, yet indeterminate, 4-D delinquency.[12]

If the Borromean knot served as a generative topological armature at a formal level, it was also pressed into service at the level of detail as we continued the sinthomic automatism into the fabrication logic. We did this by mandating trifurcation as a basic joint property (i.e., only three edges at any node) and then attempting to automate the necessary material thickness of the still-surface sinthome form as a fourth vector. In other words, we prioritized the nodal joint and its thickness as a technical property and devised a Voronoi applet to search for arrangements by which trifurcated nodes might populate the sinthome surface according to a necessity of thickness. The Voronoi Bunny referred to earlier was the moment at which we tested the applet on the by-now iconic cartoon rabbit 3-D. In this case the rabbit was infected, as it were, by Lloyd's algorithm, which populated its surface with colored planar patches that it then adjusted to search for trifurcated arrangements.

The image of a seething iridescent bunny was at once hilarious and chilling, since it subtended a quite cold-hearted ethic with respect to extant architectural protocol, and we thought immediately of the hare of ancient Egypt as the symbol of Thoth, god of writing, castigated in its incapacitation of living memory.[19] In other words, what emerged was the age-old suspicion of new technology in its usurpation of "natural" thought and action, and the havoc this will wreak on extant protocols of production and reception, already rehearsed by Joyce in relation to literary praxis. The thought of the magical association of bunnies, disappearing and reappearing in rings such as sleeves and hats, the rabbit-(w)hole-ism of Joyce the Conjurer and his sleights-of-hand, was appealing.

At issue for the workshop was the condition of the plastic arts in general at the threshold of a digital age, the paramorphism of generative rule sets then interrogated for its subjective as well as objective latency. Any one of the sinthome-Voronoi forms

12 The term *alloplastically* was used by psychoanalyst Sandor Ferenczi to account for the reciprocal adaptation that takes place between environment and self in situations of unassimilable complexity or of trauma.

was at once able to be instantiated materially, machine-code fed directly to a computer numerical control (CNC) waterjet cutter that languidly carved hyperaccurate platelets for assembly. Beyond the "magic" of formation, whereby endlessly unfolding sinthome forms were instantly articulated in fastidious detail (a sophistication of formal automatism overlaid by a beguiling "surfacing" of technical logic), a second-order selective "filter" was evidently required to match the second-order generative technique: this, since Joyce's volition-to-art scarcely accounts for the particularity of his textual distillate. Clearly the writer was setting up not only generative "machines" but also selective filters to process and sift the textual spew. As we enter an age where generative rule-based systems will increasingly be brought into play for their articulacy as well as their efficiency, and where the still-specialist generative protocols of Joyce or Forsythe emerge as anticipatory of a base condition of digital operational logic, there will indeed be need for adaptation of cognitive aptitude (or technology) adequate to serve as instigator and arbiter of such profligate rule-based processes. These will be nuanced technically or culturally depending on the local architectural priority for efficiency or expressive intensity.

Two examples articulate the different nuances possible in such parametric generative latency: one looks to pursue the heightened efficiency that such processes call for (addressing labor as work); and the other looks for the heightened formal intensity offered by such processes (addressing labor as birth). The Bankside Paramorph project pressed parametric technology into a fully 3-D material deployment, implicitly 4-D in its relational iterability, yet it looked to establish heightened efficiency in its design-build protocols as well as its technical/material logic.[13] The project was an extension to an existing penthouse adjacent to the Tate Modern in London, and we imagined it as a spiraling form that wrapped around a single living space, offering views in all directions, both from it and of it, in response to planning and client mandates became clear. In fact, the project hung in between a variety of formal and technical forces that impinged on it, from the thermal laws that limit the percentage of glazing, to the limitation of cantilever or right-to-light profiling of the planners, to the structural performance only latterly prescribed by Ove Arup engineers. By nature the structure is a *paramorph*—a body that changes its form whilst retaining its property—needing to be plastically responsive to political and technical parameters while attaining an elegance of form.

13 This commissioned project of dECOi Architects was carried out with input into parametric modeling from MIT researchers Stelios Dritsas and Kaustuv De Biswas in collaboration with Bentley Systems and Robert Aish of the Generative-Components software development team.

Mark Goulthorpe dECOi,
photomontage of
Bankside Paramorph
penthouse project,
London, 2006

>
Mark Goulthorpe dECOi,
rendering of Bankside
Paramorph penthouse
project, London, 2006

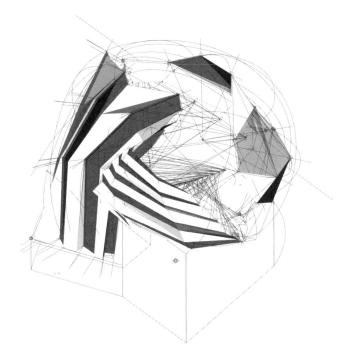

As with the sinthome sculpture, we deployed a complex-curved sheath as a base template that captured the basic spatial imperatives for low-profile (right-to-light), spiraling (planning desire), cantilevered (maximized area) form. Across this phantom sheath were drawn spiraling lines that determined the approximate position of glazing and solid. Vertical glass slots allowed views down to the river Thames, inflecting as they wrapped the tower-top space to become horizontal bands that looked to a more distant horizon, with a scale shift from the triple-height riverfront of the form to the more intimate single-story rear. Implicitly, these sketched ribbons were able to be altered globally or locally to respond to, say, variance of thermal law or structural needs, or just to capture a particular view.[14]

Within a GenerativeComponents software environment, we applied a scripted algorithm that prioritized quadrilateral planarity for the glazed ribbons, meaning that the algorithm best fit glass plates on the surface of the template, avoiding curved glass or tri-angulated glass for reasons of economy. The parametric software then "grew" edges perpendicular to the glass to guarantee that it could be installed and removed, variable in depth to allow for a thickness t of thermal insulation. We folded a lip along the edges of the glass, thickness t, to provide bearing and a small gutter, and an internal perpendicular zone for a base heater and for recesses for automated roller blinds. The "legs" were then formed around the glass according to the performance needs of both, with the local laws becoming subordinate to global control points that acted as puppeteers of each region of the paramorph: the "trouser legs," the "twisted sisters," and "the face." In effect, total plastic mastery of the form was achieved by embedding law at the heart of the generative parametric logic, such that it could accommodate elegantly any variation of parameter—macro and micro—from any of the multiple parties impinging on the technical, formal, performance, or cost logic of the project.

Fabrication was by CNC milling of a mold of each "leg" that was then lined with fiberglass and insulation, giving a hyperaccurate prefabricated structure/surface assembly that simply bolted to its neighbors. Waterproofing was dealt with by the same process, such that there was a collapse of specialist trades into a singular fabrication process. Such streamlining had already occurred in other manufacturing sectors; boat hulls, for instance, are made better and faster by CNC machining and composite materials than

14 It is notable that three times during the course of the project the thermal law was altered as the British government enacted more stringent "green" standards of building. We avoided the need to remodel by having global variancy of the glazing built in as a parametric principle.

Mark Goulthorpe, dECOi,
drawing of sinthome
for Bankside Paramorph
penthouse extension,
London, 2006

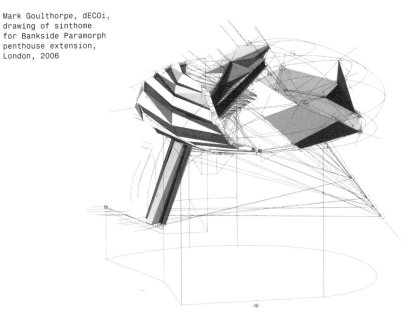

Mark Goulthorpe, dECOi,
model of Bankside
Paramorph penthouse
extension, 2006

by the apparent economies of specialization and standardization of industrial processes. The Bankside Paramorph was inconceivable except through the deployment of rule sets that were able to generate its complex form: dECOi failed to master the necessary geometric constraint *except* by embedding and propagating law. Yet it clearly attained a processural and formal elegance and efficiencies of fabrication and material, despite its formal complexity. Because of a relatively restricted budget, the economic aspects of the project and certainly parametric deployment is technically prioritized to attain the required envelope by minimal means. Such a process deploys fiberglass spatially with sufficient dexterity that no other components are required, the molds sufficiently detailed that everything is taken care of by this single surface. In our imagination, it could only get simpler with the elimination of the molding process, as in immediate deposition of particles in space, like some giant 3-D print, implicit in the logic of the Springy Thingy derivatives. In our imagination also is the creative latency that such processes suggest, which will far exceed the relative simplicity of this first paramorph.

Turning from the sketch-to-form efficiency of such parametric processes to the creative potency and formal intensity offered by parametric generative systems, the work of artists from other domains becomes pertinent. Bill Forsythe, as previously mentioned, is exemplary, although his processes are not strictly computational. Similarly, Paul Steenhuisen has distinguished himself as a composer who has concentrated on opening up compositional process to a variety of digital generative processes. In particular, he uses sampled natural sound as basic source material, then digitally analyzes it for its complex yet coherent sound structure (for instance, a microsecond of breaking glass, which yields sufficient sonic richness to provide structural form and sonic material for an entire composition). His sampling techniques are rigorous yet exacting, extracting sonic as well as temporal logics that are then deployed generatively through ever-refined rule sets. The rules and sound files are varied parametrically via digital generative agency to offer sustained sonic variance, frequently of deeply layered intensity.

Steenhuisen's work is highly sophisticated formally and wide-ranging in its style, attaining a palpable compositional sophistication that is well beyond the classical repertory, evidently post-hand-ear in its technical dexterity and "grip." It is evident on first hearing such works that the artist is developing an aptitude for such rule-based generative profligacy, training his ear to "hear" to a remarkable new level of nuance, just as Forsythe has trained his eye to "see" high-speed video play-back to manage the generative profligacy. Steenhuisen's music evidences the potential of digital rule-based systems to radicalize the compositional hegemony of classical music, in so doing discovering new intensities of sonic opportunity.[15]

For the BIO International Convention in May 2007 held in Boston, Steenhuisen devised a soundscape for the dynamically interactive *HypoSurface*, which propagates continually modifying mathematical surface effects in response to sound and movement input from an audience. The challenge he undertook was not to devise a singular sophisticated musical piece in the manner of his typical set-piece compositions but to create "the possibility of" a soundscape: to allow the latency of the rule set to "be" the piece. On the architectural side, dECOi worked with the artist Marc Downie from the MIT Media Lab and the mathematician Alex Scott, from Oxford University to devise an open-ended mathematical interface to create surface movement, using a Python-based software called Fluid that Downie devised to allow us to embed deforming series of effects in response to user input. We used parameters of "anger" (volume/speed) and "perversity" (distortion/anomaly) to permit (as in the Bankside Paramorph) a quite simple and intuitive macrocontrol to govern the local parameters (which otherwise become distracting). In other words, as a voice trigger is received it is analyzed for volume and distortion, which determines what type of mathematical expression is called up from a given set, volume (anger) increasing the amplitude of an affect, distortion (perversity) triggering a correspondingly distorted variant of the base expression; for instance, a simple concentric droplet distorts into a nonconcentric smoke ring.

In response to such qualitative mathematical agency, Steenhuisen devised a sonic interface that would qualitatively assess input (from microphones or cameras) and combine, according to parametric rule sets, processed sounds drawn from seven hundred natural samples arranged in sets from "dry" (nonprocessed) to "wet" (highly processed). The samples began with water, then moved on to wood, frogs, roosters, horses, cows, breathing, guttural language, words, and, finally, poetry. The sounds and words were strictly controlled by a biogenetic thematic that dictated, for instance, the "mitosis" of sound separation, or the homophonic constraint of words to "sound like" "CG=TA," the base structural logic of DNA. In other words, there was a tight thematic "filter" such as the one we craved for the sinthome sculpture,

15 Paul Steenhuisen wrote about his creative process for a piece called "Wonder," which was submitted as part of his doctoral work at the University of Montreal. The author has come to understand Steenhuisen's creative techniques through various collaborative projects, as well as by attending numerous lectures he has given at MIT.

Mark Goulthorpe, dECOi, saterjet aluminum Alusion panels, 2006

which by now is a well-rehearsed component of Steenhuisen's
formative process.

The resulting sound/movement environment, spawned by
the input of the conference attendees, evidenced a real-time composition machine: sophisticated rule sets that offered generative
(creative) agency to anyone. People were engaged at once by the
autoerotic potency (this seemed to be the lure) as well as by the
beguiling sonic intensity of implicitly understood but unassimilably
complex "affects": a trauma machine of endlessly escaping intensity but also an infrastructure that works so well that they could
be creative. Microphone input was used, as there were too many
bodies to allow for controlled movement input, but the principle
was established sufficiently that one might dance or, indeed, speak
"an architecture"—one of embodied difference (vocalic, here). An
inflection of the voice carried massive power as the architecture
and soundscape "bent" as a formative force: this was the sonic
Hi-D Haus.

At issue at BIO was affect, and the potential for compiling
real-time sonic and movement intensity and density, foreground-
ing the cultural and formal potency of now-generative parametric
systems. That the theme of labor has cheekily been turned on its
back here to be considered as a mode of cultural birthing seems
justified by what is evidenced in the Hypo/BIO interfaces, which
seem to carry deep import for the base processes of architectural
production as the dexterity of digital processes become increasingly operational. The Steenhuisen/Downie "architecture" then
comes to be seen as a production machine, the possibility of (an)
architecture, ushered in as a new formal latency. The author characterizes this as a strain in the double sense that it marks a birth
strain toward a new level of formal intensity, a latency of mind, but
also that it is an imminent viral proclivity in production, a conta-
gious strain of a new technicity that it seems may have a powerful
impact on architectural labor.

Valuing Material Comprehension
James Carpenter

Our fine arts were developed, and their types and uses established, in times very different from the present, by men whose
power of action upon things was insignificant in comparison with
ours. But the amazing growth of our techniques, the adaptability
and precision they have attained, the ideas and habits they are
creating, make it a certainty that profound changes are impend-
ing in the ancient craft of the Beautiful. In all the arts there is
a physical component, which can no longer be considered or
treated as it used to be, which cannot remain unaffected by our
modern knowledge and power. For the last twenty years neither
matter nor space nor time has been what it was from time immemorial. We must expect great innovations to transform the entire
technique of the arts, thereby affecting artistic invention itself
and perhaps even bringing about an amazing change in our very
notion of art.
–Paul Valéry

In its simplest definition, *craft* refers to an occupation that requires
a special skill. In the context of the building industry and labor,
craft can be said to relate primarily to materials and their innovative manufacture, fabrication, and installation. Craft involves an
understanding of a material's technical attributes, from its variable
composition and structural behavior to its phenomenological life.
Consequently, craft necessitates a deep knowledge of a material's
permutations. Glass, for example, has revealed the alchemical
nature inherent in many materials. It can exist in a multitude of
forms and address a multitude of functions. Yet when we look
at the use of glass in architecture today, we see that it has been
reduced almost entirely to a single product—float glass—the qualities of which could be described as limited, if not inferior. Craftsmanship, as it applies to glass in architecture, is currently found
only in secondary treatments to float glass, such as lamination,
coatings, and so on. The base knowledge of the material within the
building industry has, for all intents and purposes, been lost.
    This loss of materials knowledge is not exclusive to the
medium of glass: it characterizes our comprehension of almost all
building materials. But it can be argued that materials knowledge
is the key to creating meaningful design, because when a deep
understanding of the materials accompanies a structure's design,
a structure resonates with and communicates itself through
the care that went into its creation. As Valéry predicted, current
notions about every art form have been transformed by the progress of technology, and architectural design is no exception. And
yet, as qualities true from "time immemorial" have become more
sharply drawn by contrast, they remain more necessary than ever,

grounding us in a world of unrestrained and superficially informed formal exploration.

Since the Industrial Revolution, craft has diverged from the realm of building, and the term now has an almost negative connotation: the architect does not consider him- or herself a craftsperson. The imagination and knowledge of the craftsman has been only partially replaced by that of the materials expert, the engineer, the architect, and even the artist. Most of the materials and codified structural shapes—angles, tees, and sections—that today's designers and architects work with have their origins in technologies invented in the nineteenth and early twentieth centuries, and it could be argued that these material forms were not only designed for the purposes of structure and form but also to the limitations of mass production and industrial manufacturing. It remains to be seen whether manufacturing methods will be able to match the real implications of digital design and production, and so the craft of digital technology may lie in the development of a completely new family of materials that can match the computer's ability to comprehensively integrate every aspect of architectural design with construction. Although these materials may be emerging, a lag exists between the transformative potential of this new technology and the material and construction techniques applied to executing those designs. Can the dichotomy of technology and materials be resolved? If there is no impetus to tackle this problem, what will become of craft?

At present, architecture relies on a fragmented idea of craft, resulting in the streamlining of production, fabrication, and installation processes. In order to build efficient structures, designers rely on a narrow range of standard practices; venturing outside this range requires consultation with experts. In this context, craft resides in the techniques and skills of cooperation, because no one partner in this collaboration can achieve the high level of exploration that used to be attained by the individual craftsmen who operated in the conventions of their time.

Mastering the sheer depth of materials understanding and corresponding techniques certainly poses a challenge, but architectural education has to date made very little attempt to put materials knowledge at its core. This problem is not exclusive to architectural pedagogy—it is shared and perpetuated by related disciplines. So-called craft programs, for example, attempt to frame craft as a fine art, further removing it from the building trades. Within the professions of architecture and engineering, materials knowledge has largely been separated from the design process. Specialization within most of the building trades encourages the perpetual deployment of homogenized materials and

techniques that only reinforce a diminished understanding of
a material's full capabilities. This may be more efficient, but in
process only, as a full examination of the costs of producing architecture in this manner reveals.

Of course, the realm of the nonstandard comes with the
possibility of greater risk during construction, but a full understanding of a material's potential removes risk from the equation.
Essentially, the craft applied to the whole process mitigates the
risk inherent in pushing the boundaries, and ultimately is what
makes many challenging projects possible. Often, designing a
structure beyond the typical means that having someone else
build and install it is not an option, making the streamlined processes and division of labor associated with industrial modes of
production inappropriate. Digitalization of design may in fact lead
designers progressively away from typical solutions and toward
custom solutions to every problem. In this case, knowledge of
one's craft will again have to become a key component in every
designer's education.

>
James Carpenter Design
Associates Inc., Hearst
Light Cascade, New York,
2002–2006, cast glass
detail

>>
James Carpenter Design
Associates Inc., Hearst
Light Cascade, construc-
tion process, New York,
2002–2006

James Carpenter Design
Associates Inc., Hearst
Light Cascade, detail of
the cast glass prisms and
luminous accent block,
New York, 2002–2006

James Carpenter Design
Associates Inc., Hearst
Light Cascade, the
escalator on diagonal,
New York, 2002–2006

The culture as a whole is being transformed in large part by computers and mechanized fabrication techniques, and the field of design and architecture is no exception, with computer-aided design and computer-controlled fabrication techniques further confusing the relationship between craft and construction. It seems as if a concern for materiality has been replaced by a preference for the pure abstraction provided by computer software: a building, instead of revealing its materiality, more clearly reveals the algorithms and parametric formulas used to conceive and create it. This fundamental shift suggests that the role of materials has been reduced to solving the problem of how to wrap surfaces over forms. The titanium-clad volumes now being designed reflect only a superficial idea of form, unrelated to structure or efficiency. The content that defines these shapes is categorically conceptual, and its basis is not so much architectural as theatrical.

In most architecture today, a building's boundaries delineate architectural ideas. But a materials approach can bring those boundaries into doubt by extending their ability to absorb and present light information. The building's geometry has to be designed within the limitations of structure, site, and history but the boundary condition can be manipulated in countless ways to relate to the qualities of place and the passing of time as inhabitants experience it through light.

The meaning we desire to find in our natural and built environment cannot be provided by the computer alone: we cannot inhabit the world conceived in the computer, however realistic it may appear. Understanding the material world and its texture, behavior, and scale is as essential as ever. The computer is a powerful tool capable of formulating these qualities, provided the experience behind it is more than superficial.

James Carpenter Design
Associates Inc., Hearst
Light Cascade, New
York, 2002–2006, view
from the upper lobby

James Carpenter Design
Associates Inc., Hearst
Light Cascade, New
York, 2002–2006, diagram
showing views along
escalator path

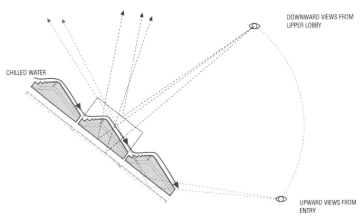

CHILLED WATER

DOWNWARD VIEWS FROM
UPPER LOBBY

UPWARD VIEWS FROM
ENTRY

Between Conception and Production

Branko Kolarevic

An architect must be a craftsman. Of course any tools will do; these days, the tools might include a computer, an experimental model, and mathematics. However, it is still craftsmanship—the work of someone who does not separate the work of the mind from the work of the hand. It involves a circular process that takes you from the idea to a drawing, from a drawing to a construction, and from a construction back to idea.
—Renzo Piano

Architecture as a material practice implies that making, the close engagement with material, is intrinsic to a design process. Making, however, is increasingly being mediated through digital technologies: today it is the computer numerical control (CNC) machines and not the hands of the maker that mostly shape the materials and their properties.[1] This digital making—the use of digital technologies in design and material production—is blurring the sharp discontinuities between conception and production established during the twentieth century. New techniques based on close, cyclical coupling of parametric design and digital fabrication are redefining the relationships between design and production, enabling a closer interrogation of materials from the earliest stages of design.

For example, designers today, like resurrected craftsmen of the past, are increasingly using new digital techniques and technologies to explore material effects such as pattern, texture, relief, or varying properties as a means through which building surfaces can manifest the design intent, often at different scales. As surfaces become more complex in their form, shape, composition, and appearance, the generation and manufacturing of material effects become a locus of design and production efforts.[2]

In this context, craft is no longer relegated to the realm of production; it is everywhere—in the definition of the geometry and its manipulation, in the engagement of the material and the production process, and in the various circular feedback loops that these emerging nonlinear processes entail.

The Craftsmanship of Risk
Any discussion of craft in a contemporary context requires an apt definition of what is meant by this, as some would argue, rather obsolete term and, in particular, of what is meant by craft in

1   CNC refers to a computer control unit that reads the digitally encoded instructions and drives a machining tool used in fabrication, based on the selective removal of material (as in subtractive fabrication).

2   See Branko Kolarevic and Kevin Klinger, eds., *Manufacturing Material Effects: Rethinking Design and Making in Architecture* (London: Routledge, 2008).

architecture. In *Abstracting Craft*, Malcolm McCullough provided an excellent examination of the contemporary meanings of craft, both as a noun and as a verb.[3] He described the technological and cultural origins of what he called "digital craft," an emerging set of material practices based on digital media that engage both the eye and the hand, albeit in an indirect way, in "the seeming paradox of intangible craft."[4] McCullough argued that "digital craft" as a term is not oxymoronic, that the craft medium need not have a material substance and that the craftsperson need not touch the material directly.

It is David Pye who provided, more than forty years ago, a definition of craftsmanship that is particularly suitable for the "digital age":

> Craftsmanship…means simply workmanship using any kind of technique or apparatus, in which the quality of the result is not predetermined, but depends on the judgment, dexterity and care which the maker exercises as he works. The essential idea is that the quality of the result is continually at risk during the process of making.[5]

This craftsmanship of risk—the notion of craft in which the outcome "is continually at risk"—has particular resonance today. In contemporary practices that have fully adopted digital technologies into the processes of design and production, digital media is often deployed to discover a promising formal or spatial organization or configuration. In other words, the results of a particular design process are not predetermined or anticipated: they are to be discerned among many alternatives and variations produced in carefully articulated, structured investigations, often in a circular, nonlinear fashion. As the unanticipated design outcome hinges on discovery—discovery that is by no means certain—there is an implied element of risk in the entire process. It is posited that this notion of risk, stemming from the inherent lack of predetermined design outcomes, is how we could interpret Pye's seminal work in a contemporary context. McCullough also affirms this essential idea: "In digital production, craft refers to the condition where [we] apply standard technological means to unanticipated or indescribable ends."[6]

3   Malcolm McCullough, *Abstracting Craft: The Practiced Digital Hand* (Cambridge, MA: MIT Press, 1996),

4   McCullough, *Abstracting Craft*, 22.

5   David Pye, *The Nature and Art of Workmanship* (London: Cambridge University Press, 1968), 2.

6   McCullough, *Abstracting Craft*, 21.

Craft in Parametric Design

In contemporary architectural design, digital media is increasingly being used not as a representational tool for visualization but as a generative tool for the derivation of 3-D constructs and their transformation.[7] In a radical departure from centuries-old traditions and norms of architectural design, digitally generated forms are not *designed* or *drawn* as the conventional understanding of these terms would have it; they are *calculated* by a chosen generative computational method, which is most often based on some form of parametric design.

In parametric design, it is the parameters of a particular design that are declared, not its shape or form. By assigning different values to the parameters, different geometric configurations can be created. Parametric variation can be generated automatically or controlled manually, in discrete, incremental steps; when specific values are assigned to parameters, particular instances are created from a potentially infinite range of possibilities. Furthermore, equations can be used to describe the relationships between objects, thus defining an associative, linked geometry.

Nia Garner, Parametric
variations, 2006

7   For more information, see Branko
Kolarevic, ed., *Architecture in the Digital
Age: Design and Manufacturing* (London:
Spon Press, 2003). See esp. chap. 2,
"Digital Morphogenesis."

In this way, interdependencies between objects can be established, and objects' behaviors under transformations defined.
These relationships then become the structuring, organizing
principle for the generation and transformation of the geometry.
How these interdependencies are structured and reconfigured
depends to considerable extent on the designer's ability to craft
them precisely.

Parametric design provides for a powerful conception of
spatial constructs by describing a range of possibilities, replacing
in the process stable with variable, singular with multiple. Using
parametrics, designers can create an infinite number of similar
objects—geometric manifestations of a previously articulated
schema of variable dimensional, relational, or operative dependen-
cies. Shapes and forms become variable, giving rise to new possibilities (i.e., the emergent form). Structural and formal complexity
is also often deliberately sought out, and this intentionality is what
oftentimes motivates the processes of construction, operation,
and selection in parametric design.

Instead of working on a parti, the designer constructs a generative system of formal production, controls its behavior through
parametric manipulation, and selects for further development
forms that emerge from its operation. The conceptual emphasis
shifts away from particular forms of expression (geometry) to
relations (topology) that exist within the context of the project.
For instance, designers can see forms as a result of reactions to
a context of "forces" or actions, as demonstrated by Greg Lynn's
work.[8] There is, however, nothing automatic or deterministic in the
definition of actions and reactions: they implicitly create "fields of
indetermination" from which unexpected and genuinely new forms
might emerge. Unpredictable variations are generated from the
built multiplicities.[9]

The capacity of parametric computational techniques to
generate new designs is highly dependent on the designer's per-
ceptual and cognitive abilities, because continuous, transformative
processes ground the emergent form (i.e., its discovery) in qualitative cognition. The designer essentially becomes an editor of the
generative potentiality of the designed system, where the choice
of emergent forms is driven largely by the designer's aesthetic and
plastic sensibilities. The designer simultaneously interprets and
manipulates a parametric computational construct in a complex
discourse that is continuously reconstituting itself—a self-reflexive
discourse in which graphics actively shape the designer's thinking

8 See Greg Lynn, *Animate Form* (New York: Princeton Architectural Press, 1999).

9 The underlying computational processes are actually highly deterministic. It is our inability to anticipate the outcomes of these processes that gives them the qualities of unpredictability and indeterminacy.

process. The potential for crafting the parametric processes of conceptual production—and the outcomes of those processes—lies precisely in the designer's capacity to edit the underlying generative system.

Through stress on the discovery of form, the determinism of traditional design practices is abandoned for the directed, precise indeterminacy of new digital processes of conception. There is an explicit recognition that admittance of the unpredictable and unexpected is what often paves the way to poetic invention and creative transformation. The nonlinearity, indeterminacy, and emergence are intentionally sought out, with a considerable degree of risk involved as the successful outcomes—however determined—are anything but certain.

Craft in Digital Fabrication

While the digital techniques of parametric design have redefined the relationship between conception and representation, enabling designers to carefully craft the formal outcomes through iterative processes, the technologies of digital fabrication have enabled a closer investigation of material outcomes from the earliest stages of design.

The various CNC processes of shaping and reshaping, based on cutting, subtractive, additive, and formative fabrication, have provided designers with an unprecedented capacity to control the parameters of material production and to precisely craft the desired material outcomes.[10] Knowing the production capabilities and availability of particular digitally driven fabrication equipment enables designers to design specifically for the capabilities of those machines. The consequence is that designers are becoming much more directly involved in the fabrication process, since they create the information that is translated by fabricators directly into the control data, which drives the digital fabrication equipment.

For example, in sheet-metal production, corrugated, flat, and curved profiles can be perforated, drilled, milled, and so forth in a wide variety of ways afforded by the digital fabrication technologies. Virtually any corrugation profile can be produced, including variations in frequency and amplitude; perforations of any pattern can be produced by mechanical milling. A very good example of what can be attained with flat sheets is the De Young Museum in San Francisco, designed by Herzog and de Meuron and completed in 2005. The large surfaces of the rain screen that covers the building are made from over seven thousand copper

10 For a discussion of various CNC processes, see chap. 3, "Digital Fabrication," in Kolarevic, ed., *Architecture in the Digital Age*.

Herzog & de Meuron,
De Young Museum, San
Francisco, California,
2005, rain screen
panels

panels (12 feet by 2 1/2 feet [3.66 meters by .76 meters] in size), each of which features unique halftone cutouts and embossed patterns abstracted from images of the surrounding tree canopies. The circular perforations and indentations produce abstract images when seen from a distance, similar to how patterns of dots of varying size used in newsprint fool the eye into seeing different shades of gray. A number of geometric and material alternatives were developed in an iterative fashion, in close collaboration with the fabricator, Zahner of Kansas City, until they arrived at the final double-patterning solution.

Working on a different scale—that of a single panel—and using CNC milling (i.e., subtractive fabrication), Bernard Cache developed a parametric production process in which slight varia-tions of parameter values, either incremental or random, would produce a series of differentiated yet repetitive objects (referred to by Cache as objectiles), each of which would feature unique decorative relief or cutout patterns, striated surface configura-tions, and the like. A particularly effective technique was to exploit inherent properties of the material, such as varying coloration of different layers in laminated wood sheets, to produce intricate surface effects by CNC-milling shallow 3-D curvilinear forms in a relatively small surface area. This technique had the added benefit of introducing a certain economy of production by reducing the amount of machining and material waste.

These two examples are just a few of the many projects completed over the past two decades that have utilized parametric design techniques and digital fabrication technologies in an innovative fashion. Typically, both the parametric description of the geometry and the resulting CNC code for fabrication are crafted through a series of iterative steps, in which small quantitative changes in the values of certain parameters would produce qualitatively different results. Just like the craftsman of the past, the craftsman of the digital age—the designer working with virtual representation of the material artifacts—seeks out unpredictable outcomes by experimenting with what the medium and the tools have to offer.

In the design and production processes driven by digital technologies—the digital making—craft could be understood as a set of deliberate actions based on continuous, iterative experimentation, error, and modification that could lead in the end to some innovative, unexpected, unpredictable outcome to be discovered in the intertwined processes of conception and production. More precisely, craft is associated with the slight adjustments and subtle changes to the parameters that define processes of design and production in search of such an outcome. Knowing what, why, and how to adjust requires deep knowledge of the processes, tools, and techniques, just as it did in the predigital era.

The designers—the contemporary craftsmen—are in continuous control of design and production and rely on iterative, cyclical development based on feedback loops between the parametric definition of the geometry and the digital fabrication of material artifacts. The discoveries are in most cases directly dependent on unanticipated outcomes and are anything but ascertained (Pye's "craftsmanship of risk" writ digitally). The designers are continually looking for particular affordances that a chosen production method can offer or unexpected resistances encountered as they engage a particular tool and a piece of material. This repeated, cyclical interaction between the "work of the mind" and the "work of the hand"—in the words of Renzo Piano—is what provides for a particularly rich and rewarding context for design and production. This highly iterative process is the essence of the contemporary understanding of craft—the craft of digital making.

Exclusive Dexterity
Kevin Rotheroe

As a verb, the word *craft* is essentially defined as an act requiring special skill or dexterity. Indeed, it first came into widespread use in conjunction with the advent of guilds—self-protective medieval associations, or private clubs, of artisans with formally cultivated talents rooted in innate and rare abilities. This concept of skilled persons acting collectively on behalf of their individual commercial and political interests was eventually diluted into the much bigger pool of twentieth-century labor unions. The memberships of such descendant organizations typically possessed a wide range of lesser skill sets, often deployed in the automated world of assembled mass-market products—a world where laborers themselves sometimes became commodified, interchangeable, replaceable small parts in a large process of duplication.

In the early days of modernism, manufacturers became preoccupied with mastering such means of production, or worried about who owned them and controlled the means of mass duplication and standardization. Eventually, some perversely relished the forced passivity of disengaged workers unable to do anything that might reduce efficiency. As Andy Warhol infamously responded when queried about the celebration of mundane duplication at the Factory in the mid-1960s, "Well, it gives me something to do."

Such embracing of the absence of opportunity to intervene in, harness, or imaginatively contribute to a mindless process of making inevitably showed itself to be a dead end. Merely having a task to occupy one's time is hardly a celebration of the dignity of labor. Glorifying automated industrialized mass production, ensuring the lack of time and space in which a worker might think and contribute in artful ways, could never be the road to well-crafted results.

So, what has become of the original notion of the craftsperson as an individual with special talents typically deployed within one family of materials? In today's business parlance, it would be reasonable to describe such individuals as those who add greater value to the process of making material artifacts. But, having stated that, what is the fundamental nature of the value skilled labor adds?

The term *well crafted* has a broad spectrum of connotations. Witness the continued, widespread, and promotional use of phrases such as "Old World craftsmanship" or "precision-crafted performance." In the vast array of connotations such phrases evoke, two categories prevail: those describing the rare, added artistic value contributed by individuals, and those highlighting the exceptional precision embodied in a product, regardless of whether the tools used to make it are digital or conventional. One can take a slightly risky, unapologetically elitist position by

Kevin Rotheroe, CAD-CAM
Process, 2006

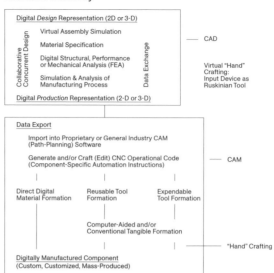

Digital *Design* Representation (2D or 3-D)

Collaborative Concurrent Design

- Virtual Assembly Simulation
- Material Specification
- Digital Structural, Performance or Mechanical Analysis (FEA)
- Simulation & Analysis of Manufacturing Process

Data Exchange

Digital *Production* Representation (2-D or 3-D)

— CAD

Virtual "Hand" Crafting: Input Device as Ruskinian Tool

Data Export

- Import into Proprietary or General Industry CAM (Path-Planning) Software
- Generate and/or Craft (Edit) CNC Operational Code (Component-Specific Automation Instructions)

— CAM

Direct Digital Material Formation   Reusable Tool Formation   Expendable Tool Formation

Computer-Aided and/or Conventional Tangible Formation

— "Hand" Crafting

Digitally Manufactured Component (Custom, Customized, Mass-Produced)

Oxford University
Museum, Oxford,
England, 1860

Kevin Rotheroe,
Diagram, 2006

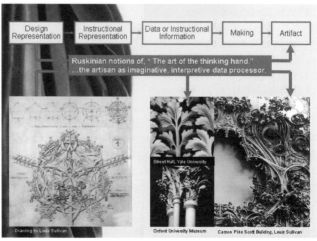

pointing out that artistic merit or rare precision inevitably foster exclusivity: they float to the top, to the higher end of any market. The well-crafted artifact has always been valued monetarily because of its uniqueness, rarity, and embedded labor. And so although the benchmark has become a technologically driven moving target that raises the quality of manufactured output, the compensating, comforting truth is that everybody still wants the quantifiable, measurable evidence of craft. But the perceived loss of craft at the hands of mechanically driven industrialization and digitally driven automation that accompanies this is not justified. There are distinct limits to the blame that can be attributed to industrialization and the consequent standardized, mass-produced materials.

Architects and designers have always dealt with a material palette dictated by the operational mechanics of extraction, processing (into a useful state), and transportation. Technological evolution is ever expanding the palette of available materials, which is a blessing, not a curse, for craft. The loss of certain skills related to working with certain families of materials has as much to do with the evolution of underlying theoretical aesthetic premises rooted in technological change as it does with the economic consequences of mass production. One could argue that Mies put as much thought into refined, well-crafted connections between off-the-shelf steel materials as the O'Shea brothers did into the unique, artfully carved capitals of the Oxford University Museum, Deane and Woodward's Ruskinian Gothic masterpiece completed in 1860.

Whether or not one accepts such arguments, we are still left with the need to consider where, within the process of designing and making, artistic crafting can take place and how opportunities to craft have shifted or been transformed by digital environments and computer-aided manufacturing. It is a question that leads us back to the infancy of industrialization and the writings of John Ruskin, who described the work of craftsmen as "the art of the thinking hand."[1] Over 150 years later, Ruskin's writings remain the most thorough and thoughtful reflections on the role of dignified labor in the creation of architecture.

Indeed, Ruskin celebrated the freedom of the artisan to exercise imagination and interpretive creativity during the act of translating graphic representations—that is, the instructions for making—into artfully formed materials. The artisan's freedom had two sources: first, the ambiguity, incompleteness, or imprecision embodied in the drawings or the rendered sketches from which

1   This is a paraphrase of Ruskin's key concepts, as quoted in Oswald Spengler,   *Man and Technics* (London: Allen & Unwin, 1932), 41.

the artisan worked; and second, the deliberate, altruistic choice on the part of the designer, owner, or contractor to let a freedom of interpretation exist, to, in a sense, treat the skilled worker as an artist commissioned by a patron to make select building components with only minimal, contextual guidance from the architect. In the case of the Oxford University Museum, much of the ornament was never even drawn. Its scope and context were defined by the architect, the subject matter specified, then the O'Shea brothers were left to select the aspects of that subject matter to be celebrated and to choose how such features might be expressed.

This is an entirely enticing approach to the art of architecture and to defining how craft can be cultivated, whether via chisel or computer numerical control (CNC) device. Probably much more room exists to cultivate such an approach than is often presumed in contemporary practice. At the same time, this supposition is enticing precisely because it is romantic. The artisans Ruskin celebrated were the cream of the laboring crop, those employed for making the special bits of architecture rather than for laying identical stones in place or transporting them to the site.

Today we would call the projects that Ruskin's artisans worked on "high-end" commissions, be they museums or institutional facilities or private dwellings for successful individuals—set apart from the work of building retail warehouses or the fields of mass-customized tract homes surrounding them. We must remember that one has always had to be able to afford glorifed labor and celebrated craftsmanship. But we can, and should, be doing just that much more frequently, especially given the rise of digital manufacturing, the arrival of machines that can make one hundred one-offs almost as efficiently as one hundred identical items. The main sobering caveat is that such machines cost money to own and operate, and they require trained operators, with this overhead being reflected in the cost of the custom components we desire.

This implicitly poses the question, "If we can afford a $45,000 rapid prototyping machine, why can't we afford a skilled artisan working with stone, metal, or wood?" While there are not as many artisans as there used to be, they are still around, often working in other arenas but welcoming a knock on the door by an architect. Both avenues can and should be explored at the same time, a cross-fertilization of the conventional and the digital that can stimulate creativity.

In short, it seems technology is a stent in the thickened artery of artistic possibility, but before the stent there was enough blood flowing to keep the possibility alive. Opportunities for custom-crafted originality have always existed. Digital fabrication fundamentally enables very little that was not possible before, but it does, very generally, facilitate the economic viability of bespoke design and thereby serves as a catalyst that reawakens us to neglected opportunities.

It is in the capacity to produce such work that Ruskin meets the world of digital fabrication. Ruskin placed supreme value on the marks made by the hands of an individual artisan; it was the ultimate evidence of the "thinking hand," the designer label of the one-of-a-kind material artifact. Digital fabrication, too, places supreme value on its capacity to generate unique output: the only difference is the absence of direct intervention of the human hand. Or is it? The marks left were made by the tools the artisan held in his hands. Where do the hands of the artisan leave their marks in the world of digital design and fabrication? Are they the hands of the skilled operator of a CNC device or those of the handler of digital data who generates the code that tells such a machine or instrument what to do?

To a limited extent, perhaps the answer is both. But these are not the hands of a craftsperson. It seems that the act of crafting something well, if digital means are to be employed, is increasingly obliged to be embodied in the virtual representation created in a digital design environment. It is precisely from such representations that the data for making is extracted, exported, and reimported into other software used to generate code for automated making. The crafting hand must be present during the creation of a fully defined representation if it is to be present at all. As a result, the opportunity to do the dignified labor of the craftsperson is now increasingly falling into the laps of architects and designers.

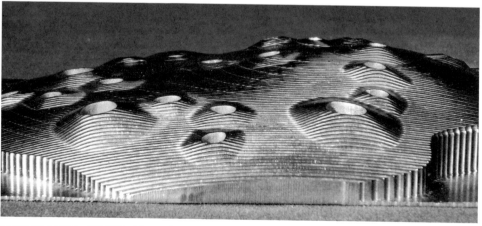

Rustam-Marc Mehta, CNC Milled Brass for Yale School of Architecture, 2005

Detail Deliberations
Peggy Deamer

In *Reading in Detail: Aesthetics and the Feminine*, Naomi Schor described how detail, in the visual as well as literary arts, is always foregrounded at moments of crisis in culture—at moments when notions of social identity are being reinterpreted. She makes the point that detail, in being linked to issues of ornament, the every-day, and the feminine, is an arbitrator in recalibrating subjectivity. The change to architectural production brought on by parametric design, though not normally linked to a discourse of detail, is in fact essentially tied to it, and this is indeed a moment of crisis in architectural detail. An exploration of these ideas involves both the nature of the new detail and the reconstituted subject it implies.[1]

The late nineteenth and early twentieth centuries witnessed a similar crisis, and the socioaesthetic issues of that period provide the terms for a contemporary analysis of detail. Because indus-trialization brought with it a threat to craft and anxiety over detail (either supporting craft or effacing it), the expressive, economic, and social status of both were at the forefront of architectural debate. The aesthetic solutions—both conceptual and physical—offered at that time, are strikingly similar to those of today.

John Ruskin, perhaps the most provoked nineteenth-century architectural moralist, made a life's work of equating good architecture with good workers and a good society. Thus, his con-cern that the craftsman not be a slave to the designer/architect, mindlessly carrying out prescribed and fully drawn details, is a plea for the craftsman's identity, whose role in devising a particular element is at the heart of that identity. If the artisan is sanding, refining, and perfecting something he had no hand in forming, it is amoral conceptually and economically. The architecturally exact-ing detail flourishes at the expense of craftsmanship.[2]

Weighing in on this issue but with a different judgment, Adolf Loos, the early-twentieth-century cultural modernist, pro-fessed a less sentimental view of the freedom of the craftsman and the need for self-expression. Loos disagreed with his Viennese predecessor Josef Hoffman—and implicitly, before him, Ruskin and William Morris—over the need for the joy of labor that comes with working off the assembly line and directly with one's hands. Loos claimed that craftsmanship is *essentially* impersonal; that any evocation of a craft tradition would acknowledge its repetitive, systemlike essence. Of the carpenter, he wrote, "Straight lines,

1 This essay owes a great deal to those whose original insights stimulated much of the thinking here: Bernard Cache, whose articles draw attention to the fact that current parametric means of production are a fulfillment of late-nineteenth-century aspirations; Ed Ford, whose examination of the difference between nineteenth-century construction and twentieth-century construction in his *Details of Modern Archi-tecture* is not just technical but conceptual and social; and Paolo Tombesi, who in his presentation at the "Building in the Future Symposium" and in his essay here is so dexterous in putting the profession of architecture into the context of the labor economy.

2 Edward R. Ford, introduction to *Details of Modern Architecture* (Cambridge, MA: MIT Press, 2003).

right-angled corners: this is how the craftsman works who has nothing in front of him but his materials, his tools and his pre-determined objective."[3] Indeed, for Loos, the enemy is not the nonmanual, it is—and here he does agree with Ruskin—the artist that the craftsman has to serve. The craftsman on his own would naturally make things "in the modern spirit," modernity *defined* by the dismissal of the need for autobiographical expression. In other words, Loos identified the natural affinity between craft and industry in their shared dispensing of artistry altogether.[4] For Loos, likewise, the true architect who understood that he was *not* an artist dispensed with the traditional working drawing and its con-cern for fixing dimensions and details. He prided himself in never dimensioning a building, for being "an architect without a pencil" who directed the workers personally at the job site.[5]

Gottfried Semper, in his *Der Stil*, proposed another story of detail, one that displaced the dichotomy that pits it against craft; he also placed it at the beginning, not the end, of the production process. The Semperian model suggests that the knot, the small-est of details, represents both design and craft. This description of preindustrial production discards the tension between detail and craft, architect and artisan; it also replaces the all-powerful, singular master designer/architect with a communal workforce. Detail here is no longer a condition of paranoic control; rather, it motivates a democratic, shared system of authorship.[6]

But this resolution of detail and craft is disturbed on another front. Otto Wagner, following Semper, elaborated on the implica-tions of cladding for contemporary design production. He, like Semper, thought that the essential work of the architect was to understand cladding's role in the larger task of construction and that the architect and builder pursued the same tectonic path. But he also identified the progressive separation of the different types of builders. Predicting the enormous transformation in build-ing production brought on by steel construction, he recognized that the specialization of trades would so completely liberate the lighter, swifter process of applying the cladding from the heavy, slower process of erecting the steel frame that they would operate

3   Adolf Loos, "Hands Off," in *Samtliche Schriften* (1917), 342–47, quoted in Bene-detto Gravaguolo, *Adolf Loos* (New York: Rizzoli, 1982), 61.

4   It needs to be remembered as well that Loos thought that architecture was *not* an art and that art only had a place in the monument and the urn. Modernity here is linked not just to the elimination of craft as associated with ornament, it is associated with an economic rationale that says the

modern way is both less labor intensive and more valuable. See Gravaguolo, *Adolf Loos*, 61.

5   This is an observation made by Richard Neutra in his *Survival through Design* (Oxford University Press, 1964), 300, quoted in Ford, *Details of Modern Architec-ture*, 223.

6   This sociological equation is not made by Semper himself. It can be inferred from

his description of the origins of architecture as being rooted in a craft tradition. Implicit in this is the now-familiar understanding that craft is historiographically associated with the feminine and art with the mascu-line, to the detriment of the former. Hence, Semper implicitly revisits this gender bias. It should also be pointed out that, inasmuch as weaving could be done away from the site and its structure, the notion of genius loci also is destabilized.

independently.[7] The independence was not just a formal, compositional one but procedural and temporal: each would form its own
working union and each would operate according to independent
schedules. Although this realization does not presume the superi-
ority of the designer over the builder or the architect's detail over
the builder/artisan's craft, the fracturing of the builder into different
trades in fact puts the architect/designer on notice: the longer
and more divided the production chain, the more the need for the
designer's detail to control the far-down-the line outcome.

These disparate but ultimately similarly anxious nineteenth-
century speculations about the status of detail and the emerging
architectural subject found, in the mid-twentieth century, a resolution in the victory of detail over craft. The control embedded in
the architectural detail, so feared by Ruskin and Loos, and the
redeployment of the artisan into the ranks of specialized union
labor, described by Wagner, became the hallmark of the new era.

One need not go into the full, complex narrative of modern
detail that is so astutely surveyed in Ed Ford's *The Details of
Modern Architecture*. But it is worth describing some of its characteristics—as well as those of the resultant architectural subject—to
lay out the mise-en-scène of the field of architecture's subsequent
reaction to it. As Ford described it, the modernist detail was the
nondetail, which is to say, it did not aim to express the technique of
construction but, rather, to promote the effect of plastic composition that did not seek to distract with attention-grabbing detail.
Modernism's concern for an architecture both monolithic and
heroic in its compositional unity and weightless in its machinelike
disengagement from the ground yielded an aesthetic of effortlessness. Detail, always the conveyor of difference (not of monolithic
uniformity) and support (not of weightlessness), was put into the
service of not looking like it existed, of not looking like labor was
required.[8]

But of course, labor was not only required, it was hugely
systematized. The conflation of a Henry Ford model of horizontal,
linear production with a professional model of vertical, knowledge-
based hierarchy increasingly organized not just the design-to-build
trajectory but the internal organization of both design production
(the architectural office) and construction (general contractor
and subcontractor). The antagonism and unhappiness engendered by the hierarchical aspect of this with regard to the overall
trajectory—architect over contractor; general contractor over
subcontractors—needs no elaboration; the fragmented and

7 Ford, *Details of Modern Architecture*, 211.

8 See introduction to Ford, *Details of Modern Architecture*, esp. p. 7.

compartmentalized nature of construction work can logically lead to a worker's disconnection from the product. What is *surprising* is the disconnect and unhappiness experienced among architectural professionals given that they operate seemingly at the top of the hierarchy.

The causes for this unhappiness are complex and more completely described elsewhere, but it is certainly related to the economic and cultural marginalization of the profession brought about by design's remoteness from production, the effect of which is to make design an unnecessary luxury.[9] But reasons lie even closer to home for the architect. The structure of the architect's office, mirroring the overall design-to-build trajectory, is divided vertically between master/partner/designer and production staff; staff then are further demarcated both vertically in relation to their proximity to the initial design concept and horizontally according to divisions of sequential specialization. In this, the separation of detail from design—illogical given their historical equation (detail being the means by which the architect controls design), but logical given modernism's monolithic aesthetic—leaves the detailer, supposedly the purveyor of control, at the end of the horizontal chain and the bottom of the vertical ladder. In a perverse schizophrenia, this detailer, sitting at his or her desk, pretends to assume the identity of the construction worker who will actually be, say, installing a window one year hence out in the field. The dissatisfaction experienced by this staff person, divorced financially, sequentially, and aesthetically from the fruits of his or her labor, results in an antagonism to both the process and the other players.[10] The current crisis of detail is not the result of parametrics or digital technology, it appears, but the result of an already illogical, ill-conceived, and unsatisfying organization of labor.

Still it is important to see that parametrics is groundbreaking because it has the capacity to dismantle both the linear and the hierarchical nature of the industry. It is too sweeping to say that parametric design collapses intention and execution and thus eliminates the need to reorganize, either horizontally or vertically, players at either end of the spectrum: such a claim has too many unresolved difficulties. But the repercussions for the new detail are significant. Because information regarding labor and material

9 For other descriptions of the problem of unhappiness, see, for example, Phillip Bernstein's essay "Models for Practice: Past, Present, Future" in this volume.

10 The consultants who remain outside the office chains of both the general contractor and the architect—the engineers, lighting and audiovisual consultants, the expediters, the model makers, and so forth—hired on a per project basis, ironically do their work with less antagonism, acknowledging as they do that they offer not a product but a service. Likewise, the manufacturers of the goods that make up the majority of the built product—such as the windows, the built-up roof, the floor tile—are completely divorced from the buildings their goods are deployed in or on, and thus they are free to concentrate on applying their expertise directly to their product, letting the free market judge their success. These manufacturers and consultants are the least identified with the buildings to which they contribute.

pertinent to assembly at the back end informs the design at the front end, those who provide that information—the fabricators and the subcontractors—are seen as players providing essential design information.[11] Likewise, because the detail no longer controls dimensions but rather the requirements of assembly, the working drawing as we know it becomes obsolete.

The interesting thing about the new detail is that the contemporary aesthetic causes it supports mirror so closely those of the nineteenth-century architectural theorists who struggled so hard to fight the role of detail. Today the consistency of surface described and allowed by parametric design is the same, if more extreme, version of Ruskin's, Semper's, Wagner's, and Loos's celebration of cladding.[12] New levels of tolerance are achieved when a skin's assembly can be modeled exactly in advance, and it takes on more profound independence from structural determinacy. And the mastery of repeatable assembly, as much as the mastery of complex surface units, allows the production of what appears to be the seamless skin.

Likewise, Ruskin's celebration of ornament as the opportunity for craft expression and Semper's and Wagner's interest in ornament as the symbolic expression of a tectonic evolution are reflected in the new interest in intricacy. The capacity to both orchestrate highly complex surface variations in a given unit and to organize and vary the connections of the units to each other and their structure allow—indeed, demand—an exploration often understood fully only by the fabricator, and the exploitation of essential characteristics of the software.[13]

Similarly, the emphasis that Ruskin and Semper place on "rudeness" stems from an aesthetic desire to see the idiosyncrasies of a material remain untamed in its manipulation; in a contest between tool and material, material should win. In contemporary design the reliance on numerical performance that guides the tools of cutting, eroding, and bending often is neutral to the material upon which it performs and, because of this, it yields unanticipated and often materially transformative results. This is precisely the element of risk so celebrated by many of the contemporary

11 See Paulo Tombesi's essay in this volume. He makes a plea for seeing all the players, from architects to contractors to fabricators, as participating in an activity called "design," each with a different specialization.

12 It can also be seen in relation to the modernist concern for the monolithic. Just as modernism tried to aesthetically suppress the separation of skin from structure, so do parametrically designed skins attempt to look like they are not hung onto a structure but rather constitute the structure itself. Indeed, the fact that so much intellectual energy is going into inventing a panel system integrating structure and skin can be seen as the enduring modernist belief that it is not really architecture if it is not about structure. It is an indication that despite the argument in this essay, the new detail and its aesthetic equivalent have not broken with past paradigms.

13 Loos treated ornament as a crime, but his objection related primarily to the material deception associated with it. He was not averse to the ornamental, decorative nature of rich materials, and he understood that there was no structural reason for his use of refined and excessively rich panels other than their sensuousness and the culturally justified need for them.

proponents of parametric design, for whom digital fabrication is fascinating not because it controls so completely but because the material outcome can never wholly be predicted.[14]

And, finally, Loos's pride at never dimensioning information in a drawn detail is consistent with the present-day transformation of the working drawing, where, as previously discussed, dimensioning is abandoned for assembly instructions and 3-D images of component characteristics. If Loos's motivation to abandon the working drawing was to utilize the expertise of the craftsman/ construction worker, today's justification is that dimensions are already inscribed in the parametric protocol and do not become the substance of the fabricator's or builder's assembly effort. Still, the underlying meaning is the same: the new forms of representation are no longer documents of aesthetic control but, instead, of procedural logic.

Given that it would be incorrect to see contemporary detail-related practices as a return to an appreciation of craft over detail or the artisan over the architect—contemporary practice is too embedded in the industrial logic of modern production—it might be difficult to explain this reemergence of aesthetic affinities. But perhaps an explanation can be found in a shared underlying social concern for the laborer that was excised in modernism; or, to think of it another way, that unfinished nineteenth-century business is only now being addressed. To quote again from *Details of Modern Architecture*:

Insofar as twentieth-century architects have concerned themselves with the social consequences of their work, they have focused on the way in which buildings affect the behavior of their occupants. Insofar as nineteenth-century architects concerned themselves with the social consequence of their work, they focused on the way in which buildings (and particularly their ornaments) affect those who *build* them. There is perhaps no greater difference between the architects of the nineteenth-century and those of the twentieth than that each group was so indifferent to the social concerns of the other.[15]

This, then, is the point. Contemporary practice revitalizes, through the new detail, the interest in "those who build them" and thereby offers the opportunity to readjust the psychologically diminishing

14 See the discussions in this volume by Scott Marble and Branko Kolarevic regarding risk. Kolarevic perceives the risk as it is described here, in the unpredictable material effects of the prescribed process, whereas Marble sees the risk as being located in the gap between imagination and control and hence less in the realm of material uncertainty. Nevertheless he, like Kolarevic, sees invention arising from the risk associated with certain unknowns.

15 Ford, *Details of Modern Architecture*, 9.

roles that all players in the design-to-build continuum have come to know. The opportunity now to restructure the organization of labor and effect a shift in the notion of the architectural worker by changing the means of production is too powerful to ignore. The speculation about parametric detail and its potential is only culturally relevant if it encompasses not just the objects we make but the identities, both personal and professional, that architects and designers can assume.

It is perhaps crude sociology to think of this in terms of demographics, but it is not irrelevant or uninteresting. Already, one of the happier by-products of parametric design is not only the displacement of both the master architect controlling both staff and general contractor but also the icon of the great white (and white-haired) male. In previous eras it was in the guise of the avant-garde that the younger generation fought the father figures; radical forms were the means of moving architecture along. Generally, these battles were fought outside the profession, for the profession itself was seen as the problem. Today's recent graduates displace the older generation not with hipper styles and "advanced" forms but with their entrepreneurial expertise in open systems of exchange.[16] No longer antiprofessional, they are neoprofessional: enthusiastic about being players in the profession but uninterested in the obsolete limits that the profession of old exerted. This is not merely a result of this younger generation learning new digital tricks that old dogs cannot or will not learn. It results, too, from people entering the profession after having passed through other disciplines, such as computer programming, finance, construction management, engineering, fabrication, landscape architecture, or sculpture.[17] This wide range of disciplines and their burgeoning cultural cachet have helped attract a much more gender-diverse population as well. One only has to open an architectural journal or attend a parametric-design symposium to see the difference in the age and gender of the participants compared with ten years ago. The "crisis of detail" does indeed, as per Schor, reflect on the feminine and the quotidian.

The changing demographics are also related to changing office identities, and what constitutes the entity known as the office is now much more fluid. The worker may be hired on a per project basis and sit somewhere far from both the architectural office and the site of the building being designed. In this situation, neither a vertical nor a horizontal paradigm of labor organization prevails, and traditional identities of "boss" and "staff" tend to fall

16 In a conversation with the author on 27 September 2005, architect Sheila Kennedy observed that her firm, KVA, no longer focuses on design or portfolio when looking at a potential hire. Instead, they look at demonstrations of entrepreneurial skills.

17 See Paolo Tombesi's essay in this volume.

away. If the detail of contemporary architecture is spread temporally and spatially throughout the organizational protocols, so, too,
is the subject of contemporary production.

Having said this, it is precisely at moments of radical change
that the profession needs to be most vigilant. If the groundwork
has been laid for a less reified notion of professional identity, the
concern remains that this will be replaced by another form of
reification: producing the shiny, intricate objects enabled by digital
fabrication as ends in themselves. Certainly, the temptation to do
just that is great, but it not only displaces one form of objectifica-
tion with another; it subjugates designers to the technology they
so happily look to for liberation. And if the field were circumscribed
in this way, it would not have progressed beyond the limits of production that motivated the nineteenth-century theorist's critique
of industrial detail. A much more interesting path is to employ
technology to dispense with fixed identities altogether.

Technology and Labor
Coren D. Sharples

Information flow in the design and construction process is closely related to the method of project delivery, which largely determines the architect's access to the knowledge base of the construction industry. This accessibility is critical throughout the project's development if the design process and the end product are to achieve a high level of efficiency through informed decision making.

Similarly, the method of design procurement (as opposed to construction procurement) and the architect's relationship to the client determine the degree to which the architect is involved in the planning process. Early involvement allows the architect to establish a team leadership position, participate in setting project parameters, and influence the direction of development.

Collaborative relationships with both builders and owners demand shared platforms of communication. Technologies that facilitate and promote such communication, such as building information modeling (BIM) and direct digital fabrication, are having a profound impact on the inner workings of the architectural office, both in terms of organizational structure and the nature of the labor force. The culture of the workplace is probably the greatest barrier to innovation in practice—even more than the up-front cost of new technology, Management "owns" and will defend prior investment decisions in software, training, standards, and practices and the workforce will protect their areas of expertise.

Previous generations of architects were trained in the reductive analytic methods of plans, sections, and elevations, as was absolutely necessary to represent and communicate 3-D ideas, and within offices there evolved a technical and administrative infrastructure designed to support the production of construction document sets using 2-D drafting software that simulated manual drafting techniques with ever-increasing complexity and sophistication.

The current generation of architects, brought up on the internet and fluent with 3-D software, do not naturally think in this shorthand notation, which can be to their detriment in a traditional office environment. They do, however, have the ability to process information in 4-D, the dimension representing numeric analysis. (This dimension can be time, when thought of in the literal sense of critical path scheduling or sequencing and assembly of construction, but it can also represent the numeric relationships of representational data, as it does in parametric design.)

The impetus to implement parametric software for base building design, as opposed to isolated pieces with complex geometries, therefore came about in large part in recognition of the very different capacities of the newest generation of architecture students emerging from the academy.

It was recognized that a very large amount of resources could be invested in the development and implementation of a structure to support traditional methods of design documentation, or new methods could be sought out and developed that not only held the promise of greater efficiency and control over the design process but also embraced the cultural attributes and skills of the new generation.

The implementation of BIM as standard practice in the office was strategically modeled on a multiple-source software approach in which the software tools were chosen to suit the particular needs of the project phase (concept, construction documents, fabrication, etcetera) as well as the attributes of the components (core and shell, millwork, curtain wall, etcetera). This approach has the benefit of precise correlation between tool and task but for the individual requires time spent on continual software training, perhaps to the detriment of gaining experience and developing skills in building design and construction. This problem is compounded by the unintentional result that the project team can become split into technology staff—typically entry level, with a high degree of software acumen but very little if any practical design experience, and design staff, who have practical experience in the design and detailing of buildings but are probably not as skilled with the latest software.

For the team leader, the challenge is to find new ways to guide staff and manage the design development process. In the 2-D paper-based system, tasks had been assigned by "sheet" and developed, literally, out in the open—on people's desks. The work product was visible, accessible, and relatively discrete (i.e., a single drawing could be developed independent of other drawings in the set). A 3-D information model, on the other hand, is a complex set of interdependent data, which can be cumbersome to navigate and difficult to monitor. Conflicts can arise between the needs of user groups that affect how the model is developed (for instance, the optimum model structure may be different for extracting quantity takeoffs than for producing a CD set). On the other hand, working in an information model forces the designer to think from the outset about constructability. What were just lines on paper in the 2-D world become real building elements with attributes and tolerances. In addition to changing the organization of the design team and process, the move to information modeling obviously changes the nature of the work product. There is an inherent awkwardness in moving from the 3-D model where the information resides to the 2-D output, which for now requires manipulation to approximate the quality and nuance of the traditional line drawing. The ultimate goal may be to work directly from the model with no 2-D output, but this will require a sea change in the construction industry, the legal environment, and the structure and organization of design firms.

The most profound and readily apparent impact of the move to live digital models seems to be happening in the area of construction coordination. Significant cost savings have been documented through the use of clash control, for early detection of system interferences, or conflicts. The new site office or job trailer is an I-room equipped with SMART Boards, where architect, consultants, contractor, and key trades can meet virtually and review up-to-date progress models. This creates new service opportunities for architects as well as better awareness and control of the construction process and should ultimately inform design and create efficiencies for the firm. The use of interactive technology in the field fosters collaboration from the bottom up. When subcontractors realize how clash detection can simplify their jobs and increase their profits, they become motivated to participate in the process. Combined with top-down measures, like integrated project delivery, that encourage collaboration, this technology can ultimately help the parties in the construction project work as a team with shared goals and responsibilities. Ideally, the resultant savings of cost and effort are redirected into better buildings and more rewarding outcomes (profits, job satisfaction, and so on) for all involved.

290 Mulberry Street, New York City

SHoP Architects' selected the condominium project at 290 Mulberry Street as our pilot project for officewide implementation of BIM. The base building's relative simplicity, with floor-through, stacked units, coupled with what promised to be a fairly complex facade, offered the opportunity to develop best practices for the simultaneous deployment and interface of multiple software tools. Both Rhino and AutoCAD were utilized during the conceptual design phase, to quickly check feasibility and generate formal massing studies. Later, the base building model was constructed using Revit Architecture as the BIM platform, with data for the curtain wall panel geometry imported from both Digital Project and Generative Components. Detailing of the curtain wall as well as standard building components continued in both Revit and AutoCAD.

The complex geometry of the facade, in addition to a host of other parameters—including the site, which had a small footprint and was in close proximity to a subway tunnel; cost; code requirements; brick coursing and panel weight; fabrication; transport; and installation—posed a great challenge with respect to information management. For example, the repeat length of a panel is dependent on not only the standard module of a brick, but also the window and column locations, which themselves were dictated by structural and programmatic concerns. Because the facade needed to be responsive to these parameters, both during design and construction, parametric modeling was essential in order for the design to be cost effective.

Software packages utilized to solve complex geometries are not fully functional out of the box, so knowledge of scripting is essential to realize their full value. For this project, scripts were developed in-house by the project design team to control for all the panel's technical requirements and to adjust the output, following established rules, to accommodate changes as the design developed. The final model incorporated engineering and cost data and was used to produce the form liner, which held the bricks in place while panels were being cast.

SHoP Architects, PC, 290 Mulberry Street, New York, 2008, iterative process of façade development with shared software tools.

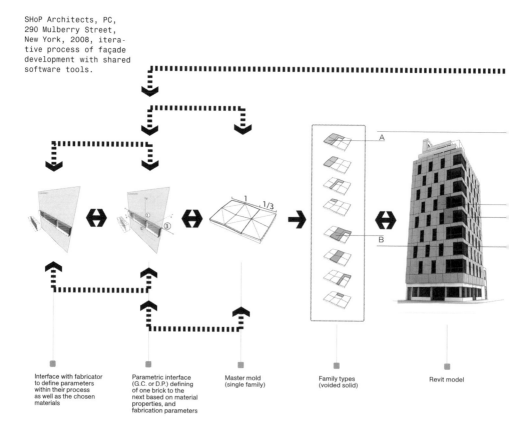

Interface with fabricator to define parameters within their process as well as the chosen materials

Parametric interface (G.C. or D.P.) defining of one brick to the next based on material properties, and fabrication parameters

Master mold (single family)

Family types (voided solid)

Revit model

< SHoP Architects, PC, 290 Mulberry Street, New York, 2008, eight typical panel types generated from a single master with rubber liner negatives.

SHoP Architects, PC, 290 Mulberry Street, New York, 2008, parametric model of panel design, with backup panel and connection embed points.

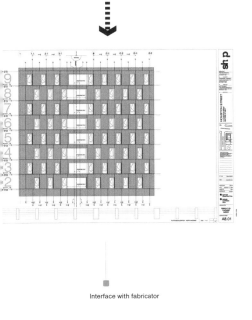

Interface with fabricator

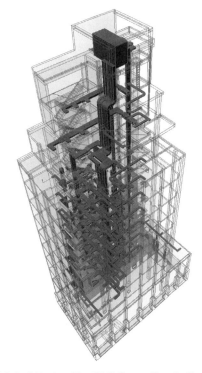

SHoP Architects, PC, 290 Mulberry Street, New York, 2008, BIM construction documents from the 3-D model.

Working and Making

SHoP Architects, PC,
290 Mulberry Street,
New York, 2008, CNC
milling process for
master positive of the
brick panels.

Technology and Labor

>
SHoP Architects, PC,
290 Mulberry Street,
New York, 2008, para-
metric model of brick
layout for panels,
with mechanical and
structural.

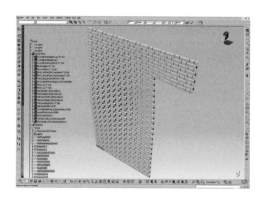

Since a thorough understanding of the panel fabrication was necessary to set the parameters, a relationship with the fabrication team during design was critical to success. Fabricators are often reluctant to invest resources in development of a design without a contractual relationship, which makes the procurement method and/or the owner's willingness to invest in preconstruction services provided by subcontractors very important. In this case, while the panel fabrication was competitively bid, the form-liner fabrication was specified as a sole-source contract.

The base building document, developed as a building information model, allowed live links to various forms of output that facilitated communication with the owner's consultants (such as financial, legal, and marketing), with the contractor (for instance, as a basis for discussion of phasing or for verification of quantity takeoffs) and with the architect's consultants for systems coordination. The result was a more holistic approach to design and construction of the building, as well as more robust and effective relationships between all the parties to the project.

The members of the design team who built the Revit model became what were called roving project embeds, training other staff members, disseminating and refining best practices, and setting up systems and guidelines for the creation of templates and model families (Revit's 3-D version of AutoCAD's blocks). All new projects in SHoP Architects' office utilize this multiplatform approach, and the project embed method of implementation is now being replicated for other technology initiatives, including the design of high-performance envelopes and for environmental-systems analysis.

SHoP Architects, PC, 290 Mulberry Street, New York, 2008, panel fabrication process, from rubber liners to the concrete forms.

SHoP Architects, PC, 290 Mulberry Street, New York, 2008, bricks are hand placed, face down, into the liner.

SHoP Architects, PC, 290 Mulberry Street, New
York, 2008, punched openings intersect with and
expose the diagonal relief of the brick panel

SHoP Architects, PC, 290 Mulberry Street, New York, 2009, looking up from the Puck Building.

Open-Source Living
Kent Larson

The architectural community has rediscovered the problem of housing, it seems, as homes-of-the-future and factory-built dwellings are once again in high fashion. The unfortunate reality, however, is that architects are largely irrelevant to the creation of most of the housing built in the United States. There is a profound disconnect between the preoccupations of architects and the low-quality, banal, generic commodity products produced by merchant developers that comprise as much as 90 to 95 percent of new houses and apartments.

Powerful forces are driving us to find a better way to provide housing. Buildings account for a staggering 40 percent of all energy consumed in the United States, but the green building movement and LEED efforts have resulted in only marginal, incremental improvement. Aging baby boomers and an overstressed medical system will require new solutions for the home as it becomes a center for proactive health care. Companies are beginning to set acoustical, ergonomic, technology, and security standards for the home office as they look at a future where as many employees may work at home as in office buildings. Places of living are also becoming centers for communication, commerce, learning, and entertainment. Architects will need to find far more agile and sophisticated design and technology solutions to meet these challenges.

Some interesting developments have emerged that may point the way to the future. In the face of global competition, manufacturers of building products are looking to migrate from low-margin commodities (such as pipe, wire, and drywall) to high-value integrated assemblies at the same time that 80 percent of contractors site a shortage a skilled labor as their biggest challenge. This will drive a trend toward prefabrication that relies on a supply chain of more sophisticated components. Many other industries transitioned long ago to lean production, mass customization, advanced fabrication processes, and sophisticated technologies, and the open-source movement has democratized innovation through a global network of creative people sharing knowledge and collaborating to create nonproprietary solutions. The world of architecture can adopt many of these proven innovations as it leaves behind inefficient, expensive, low-tech, labor-intensive, unsustainable craft processes.

An important new model for the creation of housing is open-source building. The goal is to outline a process that makes excellent design and engineering ubiquitous while simultaneously addressing the challenges that society faces in the future. This new model could create new opportunities for architects to dramatically improve the quality of the built environment and the lives of

Kent Larsen, collage image of variety of housing types in America, 2008

Second Life and Sims show computer program as virtual space design

its occupants. Seven concepts, illustrated with current work of the MIT House_n Research Consortium, attempt to advance selected aspects of this model.

Millions of children and young adults in particular are becoming skilled at creating complex, 3-D virtual worlds in computer games and online social networking communities such as Habbo, Second Life, and the Sims, and these experiences inevitably affect how they will approach the design process when they reach the age of home ownership. In Habbo, the user purchases tokens that allow him or her to create and furnish spaces where virtual friends can be invited to interact. The solutions range from naive to fantastical, but they are clear reflections of the unique values of each individual. Similarly, in Second Life, one buys or creates virtual prefabricated houses, furniture, and accessories. This population, skilled in the use of computers and demanding outlets for self-expression, will not tolerate the current limiting processes of design and construction when they are ready to shape their physical living environments.

It is extraordinarily challenging to develop tools to allow nonexpert designers to successfully navigate a complex design problem. A good designer has the ability to keep many variables in play—form, light, materials, codes, cost, structure, function, and so forth—until converging on an integrated solution. The dozens of do-it-yourself home design applications sold at electronics stores fail because they force laypeople to think like a designer. The House_n Research Consortium proposes that architects should undertake the challenge of developing next-generation design tools for laypeople that capture the experience and values of the designer while allowing for a full range of expression by individuals. The consortium proposes that homeowners should be "innovators" at the center of the design process.

To enable architects to play a role in the design and production of housing that currently does not involve architectural services, the building industry must transition from a one-off project-based craft to a mass-customization industrial design process. This requires a fundamental shift in how architects think about housing. Although traditional architects may be concerned that this could diminish their role as artists, young designers will likely relish the possibility of new and creative outlets for their skills. In the House_n approach explored by House_n, architects would develop design algorithms that would be used by nonexperts to create a starting point for design that the future homeowner then refines. The consortium envisions many design engines, each capturing the unique values of a particular designer, allowing for thousands of unique solutions.

   In the House_n model, what is referred to as a preference engine takes people through a series of exercises or games to uncover needs, preferences, values, and reasonable trade-offs—what might be called the architectural program. The consortium has tested various strategies to establish the design criteria: a spatial diagramming exercise to establish relationships between spaces; an exercise to list the objects contained in each room (by dropping objects into a packing box); and an activity sequence where the individual would, for example, chart his or her morning routine. Each of these exercises generates criteria that can be used to assemble a design for the user.

<
Hong Kong apartments
showing the variety of
additions.

>
House_n Research
Consortium Process
Diagram, Department
of Architecture
Massachusetts Institute
of Technology, 2006.

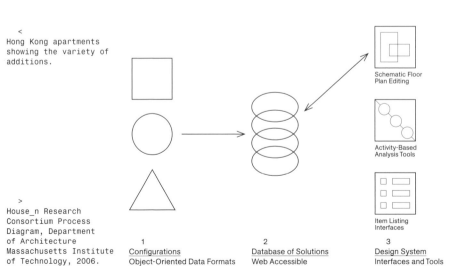

Schematic Floor
Plan Editing

Activity-Based
Analysis Tools

Item Listing
Interfaces

1
Configurations
Object-Oriented Data Formats

2
Database of Solutions
Web Accessible

3
Design System
Interfaces and Tools

A design engine makes use of this personal information to assemble a starting-point proposal that can then be reviewed and refined. This design engine may initially be a decision tree that creates a tailored assembly of preconfigured, interoperable components. Alternatively, an internet design search engine could make use of this information to search for best-fit solutions globally. Searching is well known to many web users, so it is ideally suited to nonexperts, unlike a modeling environment, which requires them to think like a designer. Searching is also an iterative process that encourages people to reflect on their query when they observe the results that come back. Ultimately, a design engine may deploy emerging strategies such as genetic algorithms that create unique and surprising solutions, although such systems are many years away from being useful.

Working with this starting-point design, the lay designer would reflect on and refine the design using one of many possible interfaces. At the point of decision, users may receive just-in-time information about form, finishes, light, cost, carbon footprint, appliances, performance, durability, technologies, and services. While iteratively exploring a design solution, most lay designers will require feedback from experts related to best practices, building codes, and design integrity. Computational critics can provide this feedback as incremental changes are made to the design. The consortium tested various strategies by prototyping both a virtual and physical design interface.

<
House_n Research Consortium user interface demonstration, Department of Architecture Massachusetts Institute of Technology, 2006

>
House_n Research Consortium, perspective renderings, Department of Architecture Massachusetts Institute of Technology, 2006

Using a design interface table, laypeople can experiment with
alternative designs and evaluate a complex mix of elements,
including form, finishes, lighting, health technologies, appliances,
comfort systems, and services. The consortium's prototype
deployed four media to help users understand the design and
its implications:

Conceptual Views
Diagrammatic floor plans show the relationship of spaces
and elements.

Tangible Objects
Optically tagged physical-scale objects are placed on the plan.
These objects provide the means to move architectural elements
and furniture to study alternate arrangements. The views of the
design are updated by moving a physical-scale figure.

Perceptual Views
As the physical objects are moved, a 10-foot-high (3 meter)
projected perspective rendering showing form, light, and materials
is updated in real time.

Data Visualization
Alternatives can be evaluated according to cost, performance,
durability, and so forth, using data provided directly from
manufacturers.

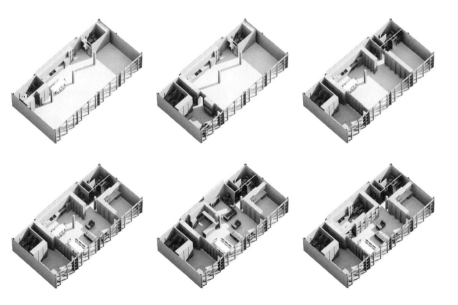

In addition to physical interfaces, the consortium has prototyped a web-based interface that offers similar functionality but that is tailored to young adults. Working with a starting-point design, users manipulate pixel-art representations of the components in a similar fashion to the tangible objects of the design interface table. In this implementation, only those solutions that conform to design rules established by the architect are allowed.

But design engines and interfaces are only marginally useful without a dramatic reinvention of how we assemble environments. The consortium proposes that residential buildings in the future consist of a building chassis, interior infill, and responsive facades—each produced by a series of suppliers of integrated components, analogous to how mass-customized desktop computers, airliners, and automobiles are assembled today.

The chassis consists of the standardized bones and circulation of a building, which may be arranged in an agile way in response to site conditions. A chassis design was developed for a mid-rise, urban-infill condominium project in Cambridge, Massachusetts. The open loft apartments were created by stacking volumetric steel and concrete modules of dimensions that are optimized to be efficiently transported down highways. Each is complete with structure, ductwork, power, signal, plumbing connections, mechanical attachments for infill, HVAC systems, floor finishes, and ceiling finishes.

At the point of sale, the buyer then engages in a design process to define the integrated interior. In the House_n model of apartment interior design, multiple manufacturers compete to offer a wide variety of fit-out components that replace conventional interior framing, drywall, and finish elements. The components integrate power, communication, and lighting systems with environmental sensing. Component types include reconfigurable dividers, storage/organizing units, and special-purpose components for work, education, and entertainment.

A variation of the infill system was developed by the House_n group to create an apartment-scale research environment, the PlaceLab, to study the interaction of people with emerging technology. The PlaceLab interior consists largely of prefabricated cabinetry that houses sensing, communication media, lighting, and control systems. If developed into a commercial, customizable interior fit-out system, complex technologies could be preinstalled in prefabricated interior components in homes, minimizing problematic field labor and allowing for nondisruptive upgrades and changes. Responsive facades are integrated exterior components connected via standardized mechanical, power, and data attachments (comparable to a USB port) to the chassis of

Urban-infill condominium project in Cambridge, Massachusetts, House_n Research Consortium, Department of Architecture Massachusetts Institute of Technology, 2006.

Urban-infill condominium project in Cambridge, Massachusetts, showing loft configurations, House_n Research Consortium, Department of Architecture Massachusetts Institute of Technology, 2006.

Urban-infill condominium project in Cambridge, Massachusetts, rendering, House_n Research Consortium, Department of Architecture Massachusetts Institute of Technology, 2006.

the building. These facade components respond to the environmental context of a building. In the prototypical condominium project in Cambridge, the consortium facade system includes wind and solar sensors to tune the heat gain, shading, and glare in response to environmental conditions and occupant activities. Ideally a network of suppliers would evolve to offer interoperable, multifunctional facade component systems; active solar shading; building-integrated photovoltaics; controlled solar gain combined with thermal mass; high-performance air conditioning coordinated with passive and active ventilation, heat exchange, and exhaust; and tuned natural lighting with glare control. Just as electrical engineering is unnecessary when adding a peripheral device to a computer, HVAC engineering should no longer be needed when configuring a responsive facade component for a particular building on a particular site.

The previously mentioned shortage of skilled labor, cited by a majority of building contractors, has prompted these innovations. In spite of this, we continue to accept astonishingly inefficient labor-related processes as the norm. If cars were to be built the way buildings are, dozens of trucks would deliver raw materials to your driveway—a pile of plastic parts, rolls of sheet metal, spools

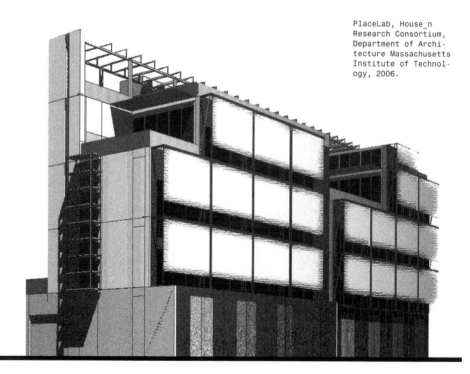

PlaceLab, House_n Research Consortium, Department of Architecture Massachusetts Institute of Technology, 2006.

of wire, boxes of screws, pistons, a fuel gauge, and other components. A series of day laborers from local companies would arrive
to cobble together your vehicle in the rain. If the car failed to run,
you would have little recourse but to beg the local subcontractor
to send out a worker to attempt to fix the problem. The untenable
nature of this production system is obvious, and yet this is how we
create a modern American house.

Eventually, design and construction processes will catch up
with those of other industries. Large, well-capitalized manufacturers will produce integrated assemblies that connect according to
industry standards. Powerful computational tools will be used by
skilled designers to create home configuration tools for laypeople.
For new construction, low-skilled builders and subcontractors will
largely disappear, to be replaced by sophisticated integrators,
assemblers, and service companies.

To support a participative design system, integrators
will enable designers, manufacturers, and developers to provide
housing tailored to the needs and values of individuals. By
allowing manufacturers to specify their products into a system,
integrators will enable the industry to support new, service-based
business channels. In effect, integrators will become technological facilitators.

Integrators are already developing in other industries: most
car manufacturers have essentially become mass-customization
integrators. Today auto companies do not ask the consumer to
"pick your car," but rather, they encourage the customer to "build
the car of your dreams." In personal computing, Dell Computers
have reformulated their product line into a service-based system
that implores of the user to "tell us how you work." In these examples, user customization or configuration becomes the new center
for the process. Once interface standards are in place, comparable
strategies will eventually evolve in the housing industry.

But buildings will never be built from integrated assemblies
unless the industry agrees on interface standards—that is, on how
components connect (not what gets connected). The computer
industry, for example, has agreed on the USB port as its interface
standard. This has freed hundreds of companies, large and small,
to develop thousands of innovative devices without worrying about
the larger system to which those devices connect. This has led to
ever-increasing quality and functionality, paired with constantly
declining costs. Trends for housing are moving in the opposite
direction, and the industry as a whole has, as yet, failed to recognize the importance of standards.

In the highly fragmented world of design and construction,
no Microsoft exists to impose a proprietary standard. The only

workable solution is the development of open standards roughly equivalent to those currently evolving within the open-source software industry. The world of architecture needs a global network of designers, manufacturers, and assemblers who incrementally propose and refine standards and solutions for how building components are described computationally and connected virtually and physically.

The emergence of building information modeling tools is encouraging, and a number of popular software packages use an object-oriented data format well suited to the placement of components that manufacturers develop using standardized data and attachments. Because the object-oriented representations can be shared directly, manufacturers can contribute to a centralized, web-accessible library of components upon which complete design systems may be built. This allows manufacturers to tap directly into the existing market for mass customization, simply by loading their products into the library. This development may help create a path to market for innovative products.

At the moment, building networks are complex and difficult to install, maintain, and expand. In the future, networks will be self-configuring, self-maintaining, easily adaptable, and expandable. They will require no complex programming; nor will they rely on a central computer. They will promote error-proof construction as they become one of many disentangled layers of a building. Homes that can automatically determine what occupants are doing, using environmental sensors, will enable a new class of innovative, home-based services. These sensors will facilitate new learning environments, security systems, lighting and HVAC controls, energy management devices, and personal communication tools, as well as promote more effective and responsive appliances and device interfaces.

Architecture and construction are decades behind other industries in the deployment of innovation. Housing is an industry that time forgot. This was not always so. The great architects of the early twentieth century, in response to the dismal conditions of tenement slums in European cities, focused much of their energy on reinventing housing. With passionate commitment, they imagined that the new tools of their epoch—electricity, steel, concrete, plate glass, mass production, and fresh ideas about design—could be used to transform society for the better. The industry today desperately needs a comparable commitment to address looming societal problems by taking advantage of the new tools of our epoch: inexpensive computation, almost-free electronics, the internet, high-performance materials, and new design, fabrication, and supply chain technologies.

Exciting opportunities exist for architects to fundamentally reinvent the process of design and fabrication and to reenvision the integration of technology into the home to make housing responsive both to the needs and values of its occupants and to the demographic, health, and energy challenges of society. In the process of dramatically improving the quality of the built environment, we may even create a more central and meaningful role for the architect today.

Working and Making

Collaboration

On the Cultural Separation of Design Labor
Paolo Tombesi

**The business of the architect is to make the designs and esti-
mates, to direct the works and to measure and value the different
parts; he is the intermediate agent between the employer, whose
honor and interest he is to study, and the mechanic, whose rights
he is to defend. His situation implies great trust; he is responsible for the mistakes, negligences, and ignorances of those he
employs; and above all, he is to take care that the workmen's bills
do not exceed his own estimates. If these are the duties of the
architect, with what propriety can his situation and that of the
builder, or the contractor be united?**
–John Soane

The word *labor* (from the Latin *laborem*, meaning "distress, toil,
trouble") denotes at once semantically different but logically
connected concepts: the expenditure of mental or physical effort,
the human activity providing goods and services in an economy,
the socioeconomic group comprising those who work for wages,
and the work of those employed in the production process. Any
attempt to recast the idea and function of labor in architecture
must deal with this multiplicity of meanings while articulating how
the underlying subjects implicit in them connect to the converging
advances in technology and the consequent reorganization of
the production process in construction. Discussing labor in this
context entails investigating conditions of work, resulting artifacts,
ideas of the design worker, and the terms of authority and
authorship.
    Ambitions, of course, carry challenges, and in this case at
least two can be flagged. The first consists of establishing a common discursive platform out of perspectives (and corresponding
vocabularies) that may be perfectly valid in their own right but are
culturally distant from one another. The second concerns the ability of this very discussion to provide the depth required to gauge
the structural impact (or lack thereof) of the characters analyzed
and the scenario put forth.
    It is necessary to highlight some of the conceptual hurdles
that could be encountered in setting up the dialogue on labor and
to outline strategies for overcoming such hurdles The adoption
of these strategies could lead to the development of an inclusive
framework recasting not only labor but, more generally, an
approach to architectural practice as a scholarly discipline.

Design Labor and Architectural Production
One of the elements that characterizes the current discussion on
the procurement of building design is the recognition (at times,
the celebration) of its expanded—and ostensibly expanding—social

structure. Architecture, as we know, is today produced by multiple players—architects, engineers, fabricators, contractors, construction managers, technical consultants, and their staffs, who collaborate, make different artifacts, bring their specific knowledge to the design process, and increase the technical content of the production endeavor.

One is, of course, entitled to wonder what "producing architecture" means exactly and whether it refers to the production of the building, the production of the ideas that go into defining the building, or the production of the information artifacts that are used to instruct and monitor the process of building. Indeed, architectural culture has always found it difficult reaching clarity on this, partly because of the objectively ambiguous nature of services in the production process and partly because of the struggle, altogether peculiar to the discipline, in reconciling the intellectual nature of professional work with the economic aspects of the metier.

On the one hand, there is no doubt that design can be conceived of as a composite physical product consisting of multiple information artifacts, the goal of which is to solidify ideas into the various types of documentation required to evaluate, transfer, and control them. This product entails a process of production and therefore the strategic deployment of capital resources, including labor-related ones.

On the other hand, as a profession that built its social-agency function on its liberal traits—that is, being a free intellectual occupation based on individual performance, unencumbered by material wants and thus worthy of trust as an intermediary between clients and executors—architecture has always had a tendency to separate its intangible components from the vocational dimension of the work. The emphasis of the architect's function is indeed placed, perhaps justly so, on the nature of the advice that comes from the responsible application of cultivated knowledge rather than on the employment structure required to organize the formatting of such knowledge and to produce adequate supports for its transfer. With the production aspects never considered a defining feature of the profession, the term *labor* has been used and is still used loosely in the cultural debate in architecture, more in association with materials and building crafts (and now technology) than wage-centered relationships, and generally for ideological rather than analytical purposes.

For this reason a first, necessary step in setting up a discussion around labor is to add precision to the vocabulary of contemporary architectural work by verifying various definitions concerning production. Yet reaching agreement on the meanings of roles, artifacts, and tools in design is one thing; being able to draw a coherent picture of an allegedly changing sector from a series of snapshots is another. For this to happen, the representation of practice must be connected to the rest of the building industry, with its points of pressure, technical linkages, and areas of opportunity, so as to catch not only the winds of change but also the overall turbulence created in, or absorbed by, the system. This is where things get difficult, since the apparently limited interest in discussing the structure of production in the architectural office finds an appropriate counterpart in the structural absence of a proper discourse on the division of design labor in the building process in general.

In part, this could be a legacy of the path of professional development in architecture. From architecture's beginnings as a modern profession, in fact, its institutions have been interested in depicting the building process as organized around the concentrated allocation of functions with specific social actors. Since trades, contractors, and developers had a strong operative and decisional presence in such a process, a way had to be found to argue for the social necessity of the architect's role and to account for the actual spread of responsibilities without attaching it to a release of expertise. Hence, authority on the subject of architecture had to be connected with authority over the operations of the building process. This could only happen by promoting, as John Soane famously did in the late eighteenth century, a principle of noncompatibility between the production of advice (i.e., design) and the production of goods (i.e., construction) and by concentrating the design function with architects insofar as they were professional.

If the alleged ability to instruct and monitor the work of others meant that architects found their true professional status in public agency, it also implied a technologically exhaustive function, unfolding prior to construction and organized progressively, which was to be reflected in the technical dimension of the architect's work: defining and organizing the information necessary to envision the overall idea, produce its various physical components, and determine the processes required for the implementation of the plan.

Things, of course, have never been exactly the way the triangle of practice depicted them and have since changed anyway. Contracts are now available that facilitate official design assistance from several other parties, and procurement methods have been developed that parcel out the design effort in recognition of the actual distribution of technical expertise across the industry and overlay it with construction. Yet the theoretical faculty

Paolo Tombesi, the
triangle of practice

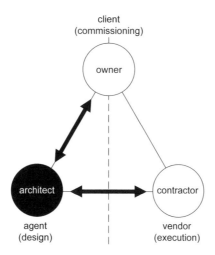

to provide overarching instructions, originally ascribed to the architect and still reflected in the obstinate insistence of much architectural literature on correlating single architect authors and building
artifacts, has left an indelible mark on the way many architects
think and talk about design—as an activity largely autonomous
from the rest of the industry, closely associated with the work (and
the services) of the architect plus fellow engineering professionals
but culturally separated from construction.

    The result is that, regardless of some analysts' willingness to
acknowledge the presence of multiple technical actors in the process of building definition, the focus of the analysis is still mostly
centered on the architectural designer and his or her actions.
Although this is a legitimate perspective to assume from a cultural
standpoint, keeping the discussion within a context defined by
social conventions and revolving around a predetermined center
may limit the profession's ability to examine its own design position, and its future, in a clinical way.

    Without a systemic view of the industry, in fact, it is difficult
to foresee and rationalize the geography and the allocation of
labor across design-contributing enterprises. It is also difficult to
identify structural barriers to design or process innovation. Finally,
it is nearly impossible to capture the factual determinants of the
industry's dynamics, which are often external to the professional
component.

The Logics of Design Fragmentation
In order to define a more encompassing framework for the analysis
as just suggested, it is useful to take a prosaic view of design as a

Paolo Tombesi, the five
dimensions of building
design

The idea of the build-
ing procurement process
as a network of design
and coordination
activities.

problem-defining, problem-solving, information-structuring activity
that, on the basis of understood conditions and rules (however
partial or rationally bounded), defines a specific course of action.
Sketched in these terms, design activity is not limited to what is
defined as architecture, however broad that definition may be, but
rather enters all the dimensions of the building procurement process: formulation of building scope, building production, building
erection, building use and maintenance, and project definition and
control. Opening it up in this way makes it plausible to turn architects' mental image of construction around so they will think of the
building process, with all its ramifications, as a system of design
production independent of the profession—a cycle, that is, within
which all the information necessary for the implementation of the
building is conceived and either produced or assembled. How this
system organizes to deliver its product, what logics it follows in
doing it, what it is constrained by, and how many units of production it consists of then become the object of the discussion.

  The hypothesis behind this move, it may be worth remembering, is that the division of labor in design is now socially spread,
or in other words has become operationally specialized. Specialization can be characterized as a process whereby cohesive,
integrated practices turn into systems of autonomous units of
work that provide particular services.

  The specialization of work can take place in two directions:
along what is conventionally defined as the vertical dimension of
the process (i.e., the sequence of operations that proceed from

inception to the various stages of implementation) as well as along the horizontal dimension (i.e., operations occurring at any given stage). A difference to keep in mind is between process specialization and firm specialization. With process specialization, the various units engaged in the process may still be part of the same structure of governance (i.e., under control of the same legal entity). Firm specialization, on the contrary, implies the insertion of more autonomous managerial structures within the same process, transforming a multiunit system into a multifirm one.

In addressing changing structures of work, the architectural debate has concentrated on some of the mechanics of these more socially complex design processes and coalitions rather than on the underlying determinants of such organizational scenarios or their evolving structures of governance. One of the indirect assumptions seems to be that the conventional relationship between architect, client, and executors remains essentially in place no matter what, at least as a cultural narrative. This has argu-ably generated a seemingly positivist attitude toward progress and an interesting situation in which, for example, technology is consid-ered to be almost a natural contributor to design and its availability often mistaken for the viability of its adoption. Realized projects, in a sense, tend to become ipso facto anecdotal anticipations of a possible future for all practitioners.

Yet, if one considered the firm not only as an organiza-tional construct presiding over a given process but also as the economy's basic unit of consumption (i.e., a profit-seeking trans-former of inputs into outputs), the terms of the whole discussion would change dramatically. To start, the adoption or application of technology and the employment of particular forms of labor in design could no longer be seen as the inevitable result of the natu-ral course of civilization but rather as the reflection of economic analyses and decisions, particularly in relation to two factors: the presence of external economies and the minimization of produc-tion risk.

To clarify, an external economy is produced by the pos-sibility that a firm (or a unit of production) can achieve a more efficient use of resources, thus maximizing the return on the capital invested in different forms, by detaching its activities from the managerial/legal control of the rest of the system. The advantage in doing this is a function of two economic generators: scale of production and organizational scope. Economies of scale (of production) are created when increases in the size or capacity of productive units (and in the volume of their inputs) secure a more than proportional increase in output, decrease in unit cost, or increase in return on investment. In other words, economies of scale relate to the expansion of the product market and the consequently lower incidence of production factors on the selling value of the output. Keeping together production units with different output levels is detrimental to those activities with potentially higher market thresholds (e.g., number of sales), since this would hinder the optimal use of the factors of production invested. On the contrary, allowing these units to break loose from the vertical sequence of the process puts them in a position to increase market share and possibly reach productive capacity. Fragmentation, then, takes place whenever legal autonomy enables a production unit to increase its scale of operation beyond what is possible under the administrative control of another entity.

Through factors of production, economies of scale become functions of capital intensity—that is, the level of investment required to assemble these very factors. Lower levels of capital intensity tend to coincide with low economies of scale; higher levels of capital intensity with high ones. In turn, capital intensity is partly conditioned by technological turbulence—a situation in which a product, or the technologies and techniques associated with it, are prone to modification, either because they have not completed their evolutionary cycle or because change is a built-in characteristic of the work. Under such circumstances, the levels of investment required (and thus their minimum efficient scales) grow, because techniques and equipment are both likely to experience a faster rate of obsolescence than they would in robust, or mature, environments, adding the costs of ongoing training and equipment updating. In this case, the activity experiencing turbulence may develop as an autonomous unit of production that could reach efficiency scales by serving basins of demand for the same product that are developed across different markets.

By contrast, the relation between economy and organizational scope is defined not by quantity but rather by the presence of functional interdependencies between activities, which make their managerial separation more or less efficient from an economic standpoint. Economies of (organizational) scope exist when it is more advantageous to operate activities together than in isolation. Such economies are believed to become external to the firm when operating a specific activity under one's authority is less efficient than buying it from the market because, for instance, the implementation of the work presupposes external linkages—that is, connections with elements such as knowledge, equipment, or space that are external to the firm's profile and cannot be internalized or can only be internalized at a cost. The cost, in this case, can be a reflection of the presence of technical indivisibilities, concurrence of scale economies, coordination of production processes, sharing of technical know-how and working skills, need for social control, and so forth.

Such principles notwithstanding, the relative efficiencies of internal firm hierarchies versus external markets in organizing a given production process depend not only on scale of production and organizational scope but on the costs generated by the recomposition of the overall extent of production. The theory of the firm defined primarily by the work of economists such as Ronald Coase and Oliver Williamson assumes that the idea of the market implies transaction costs that must be accounted for when analyzing the dynamics of the firm.[1] These costs result from the activities that firms must undertake in order to acquire knowledge, services, or products that are external to their sphere of governance: price discovery and negotiation, physical transactions, monitoring of performance, and so forth. In other words, transaction cost theory maintains that the higher the degree of technical or physical correlation between functions and the need of coordination between labor processes, the higher the costs involved in recomposing separated functions. Two tasks are likely to split—that is, result in two (hierarchically controlled) structures— insofar as the economies accruing from their separation (for example, better location, more efficient plant, higher labor productivity, lower wages) are not offset by the additional cost of managing the reintegration of their scope. Yet the optimal use of the factors of production, even when considering the effect of transaction costs, does not always explain the behavior of production systems. Oftentimes markets do not really function as markets. Production systems can organize in ways that are neither completely hierarchical nor totally driven by pure market mechanisms. Hybrid forms can be indicated in which—although the various units are formally independent of one another and selected competitively on a project basis—their interaction depends on relations that exist aside from and beyond the life of the single contract. In this case, the resulting system enjoys levels of bonding and cooperation that are not explicitly recognized by contractual provisions but rely on implicit forms of mutual reward—such as the possibility of future collaborations—that discourage post-tender opportunistic behavior and encourage information exchange.[2] As a consequence, the theoretical costs of market transactions are not always found to be real in practice.

1   O. Williamson and S. Winter, eds., *The Nature of the Firm: Origins, Evolution, and Development* (New York: Oxford University Press, 1991).

2   See B. Klein, R. Crawford, and A. Alchian, "Vertical Integration, Appropriable Rents, and the Competitive Contracting Process," *Journal of Law and Economics* 21 (1978): 297–326.

Economies of scale and scope only tell the story unfolding in the perfect world, though. In the world in which we live, and where relative uncertainty rules in place of pure arithmetics, the minimization of production risk becomes an equally important parameter to consider. In situations where market prospects cannot be certain, either because of natural fluctuations in demand or particular technological conditions, and where investments are needed to increase the efficiency of the production process, an economic subject may decide to specialize its mission, decompose the total demands of the product into stable and unstable components, and anchor its structure to the former. This strategy lowers possible maximum returns but gives the firm the ability to shed fixed costs and dispose of unnecessary burdens against market uncertainty or cyclical downturns. By narrowing the scope, the risks associated with imperfect information about the future decrease.

Dry as they may come across on the page, these concepts can advance the discussion of design by broadening the context of technology adoption and industrial change. Particularly, they suggest that the configuration of any production process and the consequent structure and division of labor are determined by a set of internal conditions, generated by the product itself as well as the potential availability of technology (i.e., the desired goal and the means of achieving it). These conditions, however, intersect external ones brought into being by the industry at large. The characteristics of the product—such as its complexity, the divisibility of its production process, and the needs of its production cycle (e.g., type and amount of transactions, information transfer, interaction between social groups, coordination levels)—make a specific organization of labor plausible and its division advisable and/or feasible; but it is production costs (e.g., costs of governing the process, of steering change, of technology uptake and labor training) that, in connection with foreseeable demand, contribute to determining whether the specialization of the process will result in the consequent disintegration of its legal and labor structure or not.

All this serves to put the recasting of labor in context. The hypothesis implied by the theme of this book is that new information technologies can be used to broaden the structure of contributions to the project, form new coalitions, take advantage of crafters' and manufacturers' knowledge, streamline information flow, and improve process coordination. As a consequence, project transactional environments are bound to change and, with them, the nature of design artifacts as well as the dynamics of design decisions.

Paolo Tombesi, the industrial context of the
building project

The diagram articulates knowledge-based contributions to the building process in relation to the
nature of the task performed (product vs project-
related) and the economics logics informing the
structure of contributing firms.
   The design functions closer to the 'architectural design' core, in theory the strategic
unit behind the process, tend to represent the
traditional consulting team, which stays with the
project for its duration; the outer functions
are those performed by specialists or defined by
market forces.

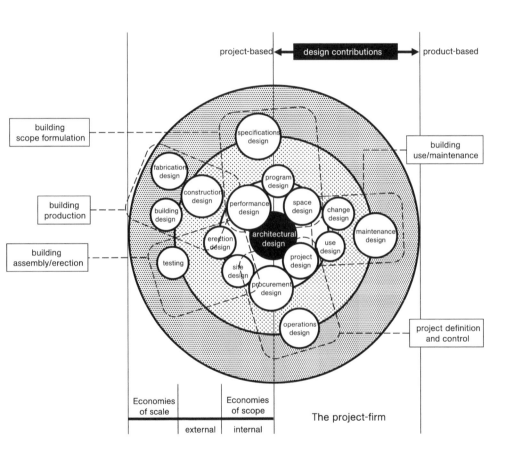

To a certain extent, this operational hypothesis can be vali-
dated: as Gianfranco Dioguardi had prefigured in 1983, information technology tools are indeed in a position to allow for stronger
simulative or predictive capabilities to be generated and more
stringent coordination of tasks and products to be performed.[3]
Therefore, they are likely to produce a lowering of social transaction costs by making information less subjective, its exchange
speedier, and its monitoring more precise. Within this environment,
product- or system-based contributions from suppliers and trade
specialists can become not only accepted but actually sought
after or expected, particularly in an environment characterized by
liability, litigiousness, technological complexity, and rising labor
costs. This means that, if predicting the future on the basis of rational economic behavior and with the help of Adam Smith's invisible
hand of the market, one would have to say that an increasing division of design responsibilities across the entire industry is likely to
occur. Such a division would involve economic subjects other than
purely professional firms thriving on horizontal economies of scale
for technical tasks developed in collaboration with or on behalf of
project-based firms.[4]

In such a context, it is plausible to expect that the linear
sequence of project-related operations inherited from canonical
representations of the building process (such as the British Plan of
Work) would be replaced by patterns of design activity and information production that more closely resemble those characteristics of network organizations; in such settings, information moves
across from different directions and not necessarily from conception to implementation, program to construction, or schematic to
detailed domains. Architectural drawings would thus generate but
also derive from subcontractors' proposals; specifications would
be written by trade specialists rather than professional designers;
design development could follow mock-up trials; tender documents could be sent out as scope drawings; site planning and
materials handling could enter the discussion on design scheduling
as well as detail design; and so forth.

Within this scenario, the traditional design phases of the
building project would be maintained but treated just as formal
milestones, with little bearing on the work actually under way, and
used mainly to acknowledge clients' approvals and budget agreements. Each official phase would combine information formats
that one normally regards as belonging to different stages of the

3   G. Dioguardi, "Macrofirms: Construction
Firms for the Computer Age," *Journal of
Construction Engineering and Management*
109, no. 1 (1983): 13–24.

4   C. Gray and R. Flanagan, *The Changing
Role of Specialist and Trade Contractors*
(Ascot: Chartered Institute of Building, 1989).

project, but their sequence would lose much of its relevance as a result of conspicuous overlapping. Moreover, participants in the project would divide and interact by functional clusters, organized around subdesigns proceeding almost in parallel. The overall project would be the result of the progressive integration of these subprojects, each containing the preliminary-intermediate-final information chain that connotes the institutional formatting of design practice.[5]

On the other hand, the very same ideas that make this picture conceivable also invites a closer look, because they also suggest that the formation of the sociotechnical patterns of work that everyone talks about will largely be a function of the characteristics of the market. In order to justify, economically, the fragmentation of contributions that can indeed be facilitated by advancing technology, projects need to have a certain degree of complexity, or technical turbulence, built into them and be developed within environments where reciprocal trust in terms of performance, or expectations for longer-term collaboration needs, exist. In other words, industrial restructuring still has an in vitro flavor; it is going to be very selective, concern specific markets, and involve only particular subjects.

Valuing Labor
Regardless of their industrial applicability in the immediate future, the very fact that the practices discussed exist in response to specific technical or economic circumstances transforms some of the rhetorical questions being raised here into concrete industry issues.

The first issue concerns the significant undermining of the practice paradigm built on the assumption that a symmetrical and balancing relationship between design and execution, or agency and vendorship functions, could exist, or ought to exist. Accordingly, domain and responsibilities of either role were defined as complementary yet distinct. Today, there is little doubt that the triangle is both blurred and changing shape. The emerging structures can be represented as groups of separate specialized units, each contributing to one aspect of the product, engaged in intense direct communication, and embedded in a dense social network. Although coming together on a project basis, these units have strong ties in place, grown out of the complementarity of their functions and the market advantages that productive cooperation would bring to all of them. Within this environment, information

5   See C. Gray, W. Hughes, and J. Bennett, *The Successful Management of Design* (Reading: Center for Strategic Studies in Construction, 1994); D. Nicolini, R. Holti, and M. Smalley, "Integrating Project Activities: The Theory and Practice of Managing the Supply Chain through Clusters," *Construction Management and Economics* 19 (2001): 37–47.

Paolo Tombesi, the
polygon of practice

The dark circles
indicate possible new
agency functions defin-
ing multiple subtri-
angles of practice.

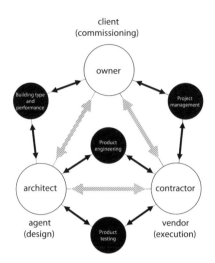

products embedding intellectual work are likely to be generated by multiple participants in the design effort, sometimes working on a design-and-build basis, who can claim both authorship and authority when it comes to specific, albeit limited, tasks or features of the project.[6]

The loss of functional clarity is not a problem per se. Classic analyses of organizational settings similar to those described as likely for design practice have clarified that producing by clusters of firms can indeed be rewarding. In *The Second Industrial Divide: Possibilities for Prosperity* (1984), for example, Michael Piore and Charles Sabel show that structures of production making large use of subcontracting practices, skilled labor, and dedicated machinery and balancing interfirm cooperation with market competition can not only shed the risks associated with unstable markets but also outperform bigger competitors by responding more quickly to market changes and adapting to, or adopting, technological innovation. What matters, though, is who retains control of the overall setting.

The literature on industrial organization suggests that multiunit environments of the type sketched out here define authority and power in precise ways. While showing that each activity is essential to the overall output of the system, network production analysts have indicated that what really matters in defining the relations of power inside the project is the value of the contribution

6 R. Pietroforte, "Cladding Systems: Technological Change and Design Arrangements," *Journal of Architectural Engineering* 1, no. 3 (1995): 100–07;

R. Pietroforte, " Communication and Governance in the Building Process," *Construction Management and Economics* 15 (1997): 71–82.

Paolo Tombesi, hierar-
chies of power within
the building project

Alongside the technical
scope of work, project
team hierarchies tend
to be defined by actors'
coordinative capacity
[1], actors' linking
roles [2], uniqueness
(and relevance) of the
expertise provided [3].

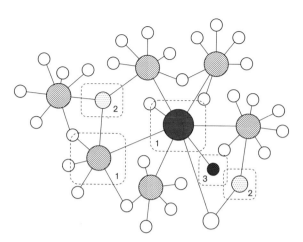

provided by each participant.[7] This value has been related to
two factors: position in the network (i.e., the ability to coordinate
the work of others) and rarity of the service, in turn a function
of the amount of knowledge embedded in it (i.e., the degree of
specialization).[8] The application of a collective paradigm to the
social structure of the building project thus implies that the recasting of labor as discussed could affect the governance of the procurement process and the position of the architect in this process
by rendering the ability to coordinate, define, and manage design
interface more important than any other task.

Shifting the emphasis from the design of the building to the
design of the project is bound to intensify the tensions that already
exist between professional design duties and project management functions, particularly when coordination capacity can be
aided immensely by information technology, which, by definition,
is not socially preassigned to architects. This introduces the
second issue: the currency of the traditional professional role of
the architect. Architects' fiduciary position in the building process
derived from the apparent comprehensiveness of their function
and the ability of this function to adjust to evolving conditions. The
industrial distribution of technical expertise and tasks now makes
this notion difficult to sustain. In a partialized service environment,
the architect can professionally guarantee only what is contained

7 M. Storper and B. Harrison,
"Flexibility, Hierarchy and Regional
Development: The Changing Structure
of Industrial Production Systems and
Their Forms of Governance in the 1990s,"
Research Policy 20 (1991): 407–22.

8 Michael Piore, "Technological
Trajectories and the Classical Revival in
Economics," in Pathways to Industrialization
and Regional Development, ed. M.
Storper and A. Scott, 157–70 (London:
Routledge, 1992).

within the domain of his or her knowledge or responsibility. This limitation weakens the advice connotation of the service with respect to the overall endeavor while acquiring features that make the work come closer (albeit socially rather than legally) to a product sold by a vendor.

In other words, the distribution of technical knowledge and the emergence of semiautonomous parties in the procurement of building design are likely to have a double effect upon design practice. On one side, the parties can well determine an overall increase of professionalism in the building process by engendering roles outside the profession (as it is traditionally thought of) but inside the project team, which behave "professionally" by guaranteeing results and by relying on the application of explicit bodies of knowledge. On the other, they could undermine the professional connotation of the architect's work and position within the triangle of practice by resizing the idea of agency and, in certain cases, relocating its quarters.[9]

The resolution of the dialogue between expert knowledge and trusted professionalism may have profound effects on the future protection of the architect's title. It should not be forgotten that the policy move for its abolition, which has swept through the UK, Australia, and part of Europe over the last fifteen years, has rested on the stated desire to attain stronger teamwork and higher process efficiency by overcoming the system of checks and balances that characterized modern construction for a large part of the twentieth century.[10] Acting professionally and being a professional in the old sense of the word may soon no longer mean the same thing or identify the same parties.

The third and last issue concerns labor as a socioeconomic group. The adoption of fragmented models of production in manufacturing has raised heated debate in the literature for their alleged impact on characteristics of labor and modes of employment. The fragmentation of production into autonomous units has been found to spawn uneven situations: on one side, pockets of highly qualified labor, functioning almost as guilds and usually characterized by high amounts of knowledge embedded in the work; on the other side, units of production with a sharp internal distinction between core and peripheral functions, permanent

9 The author's reflections on this issue are conditioned by readings of C. Boggs, *Intellectuals and the Crisis of Modernity* (Albany: State University of New York Press, 1993); S. Brint, *In an Age of Experts: The Changing Role of Professionals in Politics and Public Life* (Princeton: Princeton University Press, 1994); and O. O'Neill, "Accountability, Trust and Professional Practice: The End of Professionalism?" in *Architecture and Its Ethical Dilemmas*, ed. N. Ray, 77–88 (Milton Park, Abingdon, UK: Routledge, 2005).

10 See M. Latham, *Constructing the Team: Final Report of the Government/Industry Review of Procurement and Contractual Arrangements in the UK Construction Industry* (London: Her Majesty's Stationery Office, 1994); and M. Latham, "Architecture and Its Ethical Dilemmas," in Ray, *Architecture and Its Ethical Dilemmas*, 39–48.

Paolo Tombesi, core and
periphery elements in
the network firm

The size of the
'periphery' component
in a firm's labor force
increases or decreases
in relation to internal
economies of scope,
i.e., the level of
integration between
the activities that
comprise the task. The
more integrated the
work, the less polar-
ized and more stable
is the structure of
employment. Arrows
indicate communication
channels between tasks.
Contacts are generally
maintained by 'core'
components unless there
are clear production
synergies.

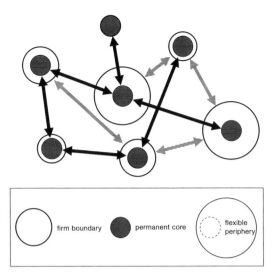

and temporary employment. This second situation seems to occur when a specific skill is lacking and the subdivision of the overall process among many participants reduces the possible articulation of responsibilities inside the unit: when interfirm network coordination is engineered and controlled by the various "cores," the execution part does not need high levels of professional qualification. Therefore, it can be managed by a professionally unskilled but technically proficient workforce, whose best attributes are availability, replaceability, and low wage levels.[11] This particular labor perspective suggests that one of the things it may be useful to consider, even for architectural firms and particularly within this context, is how the subdivision of design knowledge affects the nature of the work performed inside the office and, by extension, the structure of employment.

A redistribution of professional employment in architecture has been under way for several years now. The externalization of tasks from the architect to other parties has resulted in some substantial transfer of professional labor over to specialized firms and subcontractors. These occupational dynamics are indeed having an impact on design patterns. As a matter of fact, the design development stage—the central task, the core of the design process—has been showing signs of significant restructuring, with a division occurring between schematic design and design engineering. It is not difficult, for instance, to find empirical evidence

11 See A. Pollert, N. Gilbert, and R. Burrows, eds., *Fordism and Flexibility: Divisions and Change* (New York: St. Martin's Press, 1992); E. Glenn and R. Feldberg, "Proletarianizing Clerical Work: Technology and Organizational Control in the Office," in *Case Studies on the Labor Process*, ed. Andrew Zimbalist, 51–72 (New York: Monthly Review Press, 1979); and G. Standing, "Alternative Routes to Labor Flexibility," in Storper and Scott, *Pathways*, 255–75.

of the reduction of the design development component managed by the architect vis-à-vis the expansion of the work assigned to specialists.

Where this happens, the composition of labor in the architectural firm seems to follow a pattern. Value-adding knowledge—design and construction experience, decision-making abilities, or project coordination—tends to concentrate with the work of a few, leaving the production effort to a comparatively larger portion of support staff with lesser skills and job stability or outsourced to document agencies. Employment polarization, that is, often goes hand in hand with the steady, structural presence of periodically recycled temporary staff (usually composed of fresh graduates) or with the further hollowing out of the office.

The problem with architectural firms is not bound up with earning levels, since unpaid, sometimes long, apprenticeship is a traditional component of architectural education.[12] It is not with seasonality either, since architectural jobs have always been characterized by self-employment and high mobility. It is with the fact that the opposition core-periphery inside the firm may very well undermine the traditional layering of the architectural office, which is what allowed for professional growth. It may become difficult, within these firms, to reach levels of overall responsibility by taking the inside track, because the linkage between clerical (i.e., execution) and professional (i.e., conception) work—no matter how advanced the clerical equipment is—is seriously weakened by the reduction of the central component of the design service (and process). Paradoxically, subcontractors may provide young graduates with better opportunities to build professional profiles that will later make them appealing to architectural firms. Given the need for interface and coordination capacities inside the architectural firm in charge of the project, the technical tier of responsibilities just below the project management team is increasingly occupied by individuals who have both architectural backgrounds and updated industry experience, who maintain the contacts with and between trade specialists, production firms, and subcontractors.

Together, the issues outlined here indicate that presenting an extended division of design labor does more than illustrate technological opportunities; indirectly, it calls for a redesign of existing labor categories as well as a discussion of the professional status of the architect and its sociotechnical basis. As a consequence, the very idea of professionalism may need to be redefined based on the type of design work done rather than its alleged monopoly by a class of individuals.

12 P. Tombesi, "The Carriage in the Needle: Building Design and Flexible Specialization Systems," *Journal of Architectural Education* 52, no. 3 (February 1999): 134–42.

From the Practice of Theory to a Theory of Practice

In conclusion, the framework defined and the elements introduced to this end highlight a few important points. The first is that future project scenarios cannot be envisioned simply through the practice of specific firms or the technological apparatus ostensibly at their disposal. Selected examples may show what is technically possible but not necessarily what is industrially viable or expectable. The evolution of the architectural office, the engineering of new design coalitions, and the consequent transformation of design labor are all connected to a larger industrial picture with its own economic determinants that facilitate or thwart development and takeoff of particular products, processes, and functional profiles. For this reason, not unlike what happens in other industrial sectors, the discussion on the restructuring of design should find a way to overlay micro- and macroscales of analysis—that is, project experiences, firms' testimonies, and market examinations.

The several sociotechnical variables that inform the fragmentation of design activities also ensure that the design procurement process cannot be treated strictly or solely as an operational problem. Institutional deliberations about acceptable divisions of responsibilities, collective acceptance of specific roles, cultural understanding of the tools available, and transactional links between project participants are as important to the evolution of practice as information hardware and explicit protocols. The recasting of labor is organically connected to social trajectories—sometimes viscous, sometimes fluid—that may defy immediate disciplinary formalization but are critical in determining present and future feasibility of the structure at work.

The conclusion one could draw out of all this is that the problems related to the transformation of practice coincide not only with the problems of fabricating architecture and being architects, but also with the problems of penetrating, and somehow exploring, the socioeconomic complexity of the industry. Understanding architecture, in this sense, requires understanding both the practice and policies of building, because the way technical responsibilities and capital investments are socially allocated affects not only who architects are and what they are supposed to do, but also what they are in fact asked to do and what they can do.

Such a practice needs a multifaceted theory—different from architectural theory as a theory of architectural communication, from the theory of professional practice as a theory of office and project administration, or from the theory of digital craft as a theory of fabrication, and yet encompassing them all. The creation of such a theory entails the collaboration of institutional frameworks, professions, and academia. The first must continue to create a contractual environment that facilitates professional inter-action within design networks but also policies that consider the larger, structural dimension of labor in design-related occupations. The second has the responsibility to take the problems and the repercussions of intellectual, professional, and technical divisions into account when setting up office management, collaboration, and employment strategies.

In the end, however, it is up to the third component—academia—to facilitate the adoption and dissemination of a cul-tural paradigm in which architects may find themselves engaged in a (group) discussion on buildings but also industrial systems, on spatial semantics but also procurement strategies, on materi-als but also industrial relations and training programs, on project budgets but also project priorities. Of course, implementing this agenda requires adjusting curricula, devising teaching strategies that can expand the idea of design as an activity broader than architectural design, and providing opportunities to present design labor as an area of intellectual concern incorporating the various definitions provided in the opening paragraph of this text. As suggested, this might involve questioning the epistemology of design vis-à-vis the domains it intersects rather than treating its architectural or even fabrication creative component with blind reverence; it might also involve overcoming the cultural separation that has long beset the analysis of intellectual work in construc-tion, possibly by revealing design's social heterogeneity and by adopting analytical instruments capable of decoding the actual value of particular patterns of work; and it could require present-ing construction, management, real estate, or other enterprises that are not strictly architectural as legitimate concerns of one's professional dimension as an architect. The level of disciplinary contamination proposed here is certainly not meant to undermine architecture's sense or cultural value. The ultimate objective should be that of making building a branch of architecture, rather than keeping architecture a privileged but inward-looking subset of building.[13]

13 Ibid.

Innovation Rates and Network Organization
John E. Taylor

**"Well in our country," said Alice, still panting a little, "you'd gener-
ally get to somewhere else—if you ran very fast for a long time, as
we've been doing."
"A slow sort of country!" said the Red Queen. "Now, here,
you see, it takes all the running you can do, to keep in the same
place. If you want to get somewhere else, you must run twice as
fast as that!"
—Lewis Carroll**

The architecture, engineering, and construction (AEC) industry is
organized as a dynamic, interdependent project network of firms.
Building industry participants often look to technology to improve
productivity, but the introduction of new tools and procedures
requires the industry to adopt innovative techniques as well.
Innovation rates and the organization of labor in construction are
inexorably linked, as different components of the delivery chain
adopt change at differing rates. Significant innovations, such as
building information modeling (BIM), may provide early productivity gains to first adopters, but that advantage to a single firm can
slow the productivity of the entire delivery process while innovation slowly diffuses throughout the network.

   In order for an architecture firm to capture the full benefit
offered by these tools, multiple players in the project network
must change. For example, product manufacturers need to create
object-oriented libraries of their products that are the basis of
architectural design models. Engineers need to be able to access
and interact with architectural data in order to determine sizing
for structural members and other systems. Contractors need
additional functionality to use the architect's BIM model to plan
construction efforts such as the location of temporary structures,
placement of materials and equipment during construction, and
coordination of other elements not generally considered by the
designers of record. In short, the implementation of BIM tools by
one firm has an impact on the entire AEC network.

   In their 1990 article "Architectural Innovation: The Recon-
figuration of Existing Product Technologies and the Failure of
Established Firms," Rebecca Henderson and Kim Clark introduced
a typology of innovations—the four classes of which they identified
as incremental, modular, architectural, and radical—that described
the extent to which change reverberates across design and construction networks. A representative example is the construction
of wall systems. In an incremental innovation, a modest change to
the original approach to stick-built wall construction, carpenters
might start with prefabricated wall trusses and then complete
the wiring, plumbing, and finishes in place; this change primarily

involves carpenters. For a modular innovation, the core concept
is overturned but the interorganizational work architecture is
only modestly impacted such as the case of evolving from a
wood frame truss to an extruded metal truss. An architectural,
or systemic, innovation describes a more dramatic innovation;
for example, when the entire wall system, constructed of typical
components, is prefabricated. At the farthest end of the spectrum
is the radical innovation, in which both the core concept is overturned and the interorganizational work structure—in this case, all
disciplines responsible for the wall—is affected. The geodesic dome
wall is an example of a radical wall system innovation: the materials changed significantly and the process by which the wall was
constructed, inclusive of building services, altered dramatically.

   Each wall construction approach affects both the core
process by which a wall is constructed and the system of players
required to build it, but the effects of the diffusion of these innovations on productivity are significant. Research by Plunkett Limited[1]
suggests that the use of prefabricated wall systems, a systemic
innovation, diffused four times more slowly than the use of prefabricated wall trusses, incremental innovation. Furthermore, other
researchers have shown that the differing innovation rates have a
negative impact on the industry.[2] The slower-diffusing innovation,
that of prefabricated wall systems, was shown to lead to significant
improvements in productivity. Meanwhile, a report by the National

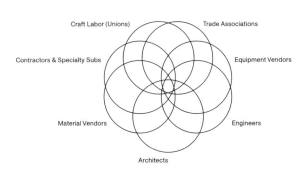

Interdependent project
network of firms

Craft Labor (Unions)   Trade Associations

Contractors & Specialty Subs   Equipment Vendors

Material Vendors   Engineers

Architects

Typology of innovations

Impact on Interorganizational Work Architecture	Modest	Incremental Innovation (Wall Truss)	Modular Innovation (Extruded Metal Truss)
	Significant	Systemic Innovation (Pre-fab Wall)	Radical Innovation (Geodesic Dome Wall)
Core Concept		Reinforced	Overturned

1   J. Plunkett, "Plunkett's real estate and
construction industry statistics," Plunkett
Research Ltd., 2003.

2   D. Blackley and E. Shepard, "The diffusion of innovation in homebuilding," *Journal
of Housing Economics*, Vol. 5, 303–322.

Association of Homebuilders indicated that the prefabricated wall truss, an innovation that diffused four times faster than the productivity-enhancing prefabricated wall system, had a negative impact on overall productivity.[3] The implications here are significant: systemic and radical innovations, although offering important potential improvements to the AEC process, diffuse slowly through the supply chain.

The average time to build a standard single-family house in the United States has increased dramatically over the last several decades. This suggests that systemic innovations can slow productivity in project networks, and this effect in turn can slow diffusion rates for innovations that hold the promise of increased productivity. The fact that these systemic innovations are being forestalled in favor of incremental innovations may also be contributing to an overall reduction in industry productivity.

If this research suggests that resistance to widespread innovation like BIM will remain high, what can firms operating in project networks do to improve their ability to adopt productivity-enhancing systemic innovations? Under Henderson and Clark's typology, BIM would be considered a systematic or radical innovation, since it impacts on interorganizational work structures and has the potential to lead to dramatic increases in overall project productivity in project networks that increase stability—financially and schedule-wise. A synergistic effect occurred when networks of firms both changed the way they organize (becoming more integrated with other trades) and adopted BIM tools. These firms reported dramatic increases in productivity: an average task might be twenty times more productive. When BIM is used, the organization of labor affects the adoption and productivity of innovations that impact interorganizational working networks such as the AEC supply chain.

To further examine the impact of labor organization on innovation, a computational simulation model was developed to predict productivity rates based on the interdependence of the task, the degree of design and construction network stability, and the number of firms impacted by changes in the interorganizational structure. Though network researchers generally agree that when firms form networks they will gain access to new knowledge, the question of how project participants learn new processes within their own firms or projects or throughout the network remains largely unexplored. Since such learning is critical to the diffusion of innovation, understanding its effect is critical.

3   O'Brien, M., R. Wakefield, Y. Beliveau. 2000. *Industrializing the Residential Construction Site* [NAHB Research Center Report]. Center for Advanced Housing Research, Virginia Tech, Blacksburg, VA.

Prefabricated wall
truss system

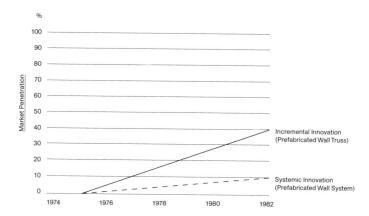

Mean number of months
to construct a single-
family home.

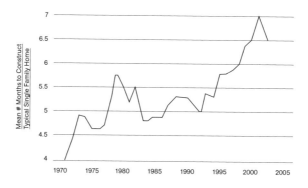

Adoption of BIM for
design and project
structure.

The prevailing view on learning in interorganizational networks fails to adequately recognize the learning that occurs at the boundaries between firms in the network, so this simulation included learning across interdependent tasks that connect the work of architects, engineers, and contractors. It also made assumptions, based on field research, about the potential increases in productivity made possible by the innovation of BIM. The simulation accounted for three different types of specialist firm roles: an architect, an engineer, and a contractor. The degree of interdependence between firms (for example, between architect and engineer) can be specified.

In a first simulation, one architect closely collaborated with two contractors and two engineers following the introduction of BIM into the network. In this case the project network achieved its preinnovation productivity after seven projects, suggesting that even collaborators who are well known to each other require multiple iterations to achieve the promise of additional productivity when radical innovation is introduced to their process. Some early advantages occur, however: it was found that the architect achieved its preinnovation productivity by the third project. However, due to interdependencies between the firms and the fact that two contractors and two engineers competed to work with the architect, it took the contractors and engineers between five and ten projects to achieve their preinnovation productivity.

In a second case, the stability in the network was decreased by giving the architect five contractors and five engineers to choose from for each project, creating a significant impact on network productivity. The architecture firm, which participated in every project, still achieved its preinnovation productivity by the third project. However, the time to reach preinnovation productivity for the project network extended from seven projects to twenty projects, because of firm-level learning curves for the contractors and engineers. Several of the contractors and engineers had still not achieved their preinnovation productivity by the twenty-fifth project. The slower productivity of these firms slowed the productivity for the project network and hence the time it took to achieve preinnovation productivity for the network. Decreased stability, typical in the AEC network, in which loose coalitions of participating firms form temporarily as projects are built, is shown to have a profoundly negative effect on innovation's potential to improve productivity.

What are the practical implications of this research for design and construction work? While innovations like BIM offer long-term benefit to the entire AEC delivery process, this research suggests that firms should identify ways to decrease task

Project Networks
Dynamic Lab website,
Columbia University
Department of Civil
Engineering, 2008

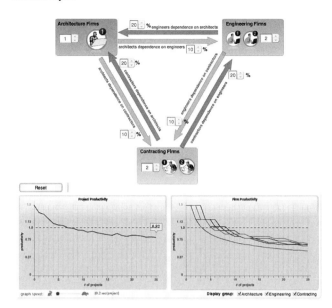

Project Networks
Dynamic Lab website,
Columbia University,
Department of Civil
Engineering, 2008

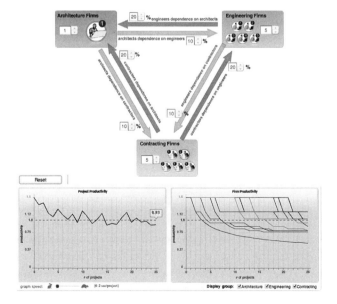

interdependencies (e.g., modularize tasks) and develop more stable organizational partnerships in the network. Networks of firms failing to reduce task interdependencies and stabilize partnerships will face protracted learning curves as a result.

The implications for innovation in the AEC delivery process itself are also profound. The traditional disaggregated delivery methods so common in the building industry (such as design/bid/build or even construction management) create unstable networks, and process innovations like BIM will decrease their productivity in the short term. In order to increase individual firm productivity, participating firms must decouple from the network, negating many of the potential benefits of this technology. However, implementation of more stable project delivery approaches currently contemplated, like integrated project delivery, will have the important effect of simultaneously increasing the productivity of both individual firms and projects network, suggesting that process improvement in the AEC supply chain will be a function of both technological innovation and relational stability in project networks.

Furthering Collaboration

Howard W. Ashcraft

Building information modeling (BIM) technology is becoming a standard tool in building practices, being used by designers, contractors, and suppliers to reduce their costs, increase quality, and, in some instances, achieve designs that would be impossible without digital design and fabrication. Studies by Stanford University's Center for Integrated Facility Engineering report that BIM use will continue to rise in the near future. Moreover, in spring 2008, McGraw-Hill estimated that the tipping point was reached—that more teams are using BIM than exploring it.[1] This explosive growth[2] has been supported by preliminary development of BIM standards,[3] contractual protocols for BIM use,[4] and related issues, such as modern electronic data licensing and file transfer agreements. And as the technical issues of standards and interoperability are addressed, the software capabilities will develop further.[5] BIM is not tomorrow's vision; it is today's reality.

But this reality raises new questions. BIM is being adopted, but for what purposes and by whom? Currently, the depth of adoption varies significantly between designers, contractors, subcontractors, and owners, and differences exist as well between individual disciplines.[6] Not surprisingly, this first phase of BIM adoption has focused on areas of immediate benefit, notably 3-D design and physical clash detection. It has also been used for fabrication, although this is often not linked to the design BIM. These tasks could be managed with prior tools and processes but are more easily accomplished with BIM, which improves traditional and essentially solitary processes. But BIM can do more.

The BIM of the future addresses a broader range of issues that cannot be solved without the combined efforts of design, construction, and facility management.[7] For example, constructability requires direct interaction between the designers and those who construct the project. Architects and engineers must learn to create designs in BIM that correspond to how the project will be

1 *Interoperability in the Construction Industry*, McGraw Hill Construction SmartMarket Report (2007), 11.

2 *Building Information Modeling*, McGraw Hill Construction SmartMarket Report (2008) confirms an acceleration in BIM adoption, although the rate of adoption varies by discipline.

3 Most notably, the National Institute of Building Science's National Building Information Modeling Standard Version 1.0, http://www.buildingsmartalliance.org/ nbims/. Also, ConsensusDOCS 301 Building Information Modeling (BIM) Addendum, Associated General Contractors (AGC), 2008.

4 American Institute of Architects (AIA) Document E-202, Building Information Modeling Protocol Exhibit; Consensus-DOCS Document 301, Building Information Addendum; Autodesk, Building Information Specification.

5 In addition to the National Institute of Building Science's development of a National Building Information Modeling Standard (see www.nibs.org/newstory1. html), the International Alliance for Interoperability has long been working on standards for data exchange between modeling software (see www.buildingsmart.com/).

6 There have been and continue to be commercial, technical, and legal

barriers that impede BIM adoption. See H. Ashcraft, "Building Information Modeling: A Framework for Collaboration," *Construction Lawyer* 28, no. 3 (summer 2008).

7 As noted recently, "while modeling tools provide significant benefits for individual users, leveraging BIM just to produce "silos of excellence" minimizes the greater potential for large-scale improvement of the entire industry" (Ashcraft, *Building Information Modeling*, 23).

constructed. Similarly, use of BIM for scheduling and logistics analysis requires integrating information about how and in what sequence the structure will be erected. Estimating cost also requires close interaction and communication between designers, contractors, trades, and vendors. Designs must be organized to facilitate the flow of information from and into the BIM or into separate analysis software, regardless of who authors or uses the information. Addressing sustainability issues also requires information from a broad range of sources: users, designers, builders, and facility managers. Thus, the BIM of the future is collaborative, shifting the focus from individual processes to project workflows and seamless interactions.

Collaboration and the Future of BIM

BIM's need for collaboration to achieve its most powerful and sophisticated outcomes is balanced by its strength as a collaborative framework. Dazzling 3-D images are the most visible aspect of BIM, but BIM's real power stems from being an organized collection of related numbers. As noted in a National Building Information Model Standard (NBIMS) definition, BIM is a "computable representation of all the physical and functional characteristics of a facility."[8] Because it consists of "just numbers," the information can be extracted, analyzed, mathematically manipulated, and combined with or related to other data. BIM data has many sources and multiple uses—a characteristic that can be exploited to create more environmentally sustainable buildings because the data provided by designers, contractors, vendors, and others can be combined and analyzed to iteratively optimize a design. Similarly, the design information in the BIM can be linked to a contractor's cost and constructability information to create the near-continuous cost-data analysis required for target value design. Moreover, because BIM information is centrally managed, entered once, and multiply viewed, it creates the communication framework and common basis of understanding necessary for collaboration. BIM's power is enhanced by collaboration, and collaboration is made more effective through BIM.

Collaboration is not a hallmark of the architecture, engineering, and construction (AEC) industry. Traditionally, design, construction, and facility management have been separated at

8   "A Building Information Model, or BIM, utilizes cutting edge digital technology to establish a computable representation of all the physical and functional character- istics of a facility and its related project/ life-cycle information, and is intended to be a repository of information for the facility owner/operator to use and maintain throughout the life-cycle of a facility" (www.nibs.org/newsstory1.html).

a professional and legal level. Standard construction contracts carefully delineate the boundaries between owner, designer, and contractor and forswear any responsibility of one for the others. This has led to a highly fragmented and inefficient process that reduces building quality and efficiency. In response to declining construction productivity, the Construction Users Roundtable (CURT) issued two white papers[9] that analyzed the sources of inefficiency and recommended strategies for improvement. A key finding was that "the building process cannot be optimized without full collaboration among all members of the design/build/own project."[10] To achieve this goal, CURT recommended open information sharing, early involvement of all key participants, and the use of virtual building models (BIM).[11]

The power of collaborative BIM goes beyond improving efficiency. The combined strength of BIM and collaborative project delivery can help the design and construction community meet what is perhaps its most important challenge: environmentally sustainable buildings. As noted by the American Society of Heating, Refrigerating and Air-Conditioning Engineers:

> The *integrated design process* facilitates higher building performance by bringing major issues and participants into the project early in the design process. For the most part, the opportunities for creatively addressing solutions occur very early in the design process. Early team building and goal setting can reduce total project costs. This collaborative process will inform building form, envelope, and mechanical, electrical, plumbing and other systems.[12]

BIM provides the tools for iteratively analyzing and optimizing design, and collaboration provides the content and the creativity that empowers the tools.

9 CURT, *Construction Strategy: Optimizing the Construction Process*, WP-1003 (July 2006); and CURT, *Collaboration, Integrated Information and the Project Lifecycle in Building Design, Construction and Operation*, WP-1202 (August 2004).

10 CURT, WP-1202, 7.

11 CURT, WP-1202, 7–10.

12 Informative Appendix G, BSR/ASHRAE/ USGBC Standard 189.1P, *Standard for the Design of High-Performance Green Buildings Except Low-Rise Residential Buildings* (Illuminating Engineering Society of North America [IESNA] 2008 Review Draft) Note that ASHRAE interchangeably uses Integrated Design and Integrated Project Delivery. See also E. Krygiel and B. Nies, *Green BIM: Successful Sustainable Design with Building Information Modeling* (Indianapolis, IN: Wiley: 2008), esp. chap. 3; and U.S. Department of Energy, "Integrated Building Design," part 4.1 of *Greening Federal Facilities: An Energy, Environmental, and Economic Resource Guide for Federal Facility Managers and Designers*, 2nd ed., http://www1.eere.energy.gov/femp/pdfs/29267-0.pdf; and U.S. Department of Energy, *Integrated Building Design for Energy Efficiency*, http://fac.usu.edu/departments/d&c/HPD/EERE%20Integ%20 Design.pdf.

Trends Leading to Greater Collaboration
1.1   The Trend toward Open Communication and Reliance

As noted previously, traditional construction contracts confine parties to their assigned roles and similarly segregate liability. This was a feasible risk management approach because the economic-loss doctrine applicable in many states prevents an injured party from recovering pecuniary losses unless the party has a contractual relationship to the defendant.[13] If the parties are walled off contractually, they cannot be sued under the contract and cannot be sued outside it. But as parties began to exchange computer-aided design and drafting (CADD) data electronically, questions arose concerning the ability of the receiving party to rely on the information and the liability of the transmitting party for its accuracy. Under *Restatement of the Law Second: Torts* §522, a person who negligently supplies incorrect or misleading information to a person who justifiably relies on the information is liable for any financial loss sustained.[14] Free exchange of CADD data thus raised concerns of expanded liability to third parties. In response, parties reinforced the contractual walls by disavowing responsibility for the transmitted information.[15] But this approach leads to inefficiency, misunderstanding, and poor outcomes, which inevitably leads to claims.[16] And project efficiency requires reliable communication. A change was needed.

13 B. Andrus et al., "The Economic Loss Doctrine in Construction Cases: Are the Odds for Design Professionals Better in Vegas?" *American College of Construction Lawyers Journal* 2, no. 1 (winter 2008): 53.

14 *the Law :Torts* (St. Paul, MN: American Law Institute, 1965, s. :Information Negligently Supplied for the Guidance of Others, §552, 3 Restatement of Torts 2nd (1976), American Law Institute.

(1) One who, in the course of his business, profession or employment, or in any other transaction in which he has a pecuniary interest, supplies false information for the guidance of others in their business transactions, is subject to liability for pecuniary loss caused to them by their justifiable reliance upon the information, if he fails to exercise reasonable care or competence in obtaining or communicating the information.

(2) Except as stated in Subsection (3), the liability stated in Subsection (1) is limited to loss suffered:
   (a) by the person or one of a limited group of persons for whose benefit and guidance he intends to supply the information or knows that the recipient intends to supply it; and
   (b) through reliance upon it in a transaction that he intends the information to influence or knows that the recipient so intends or in a substantially similar transaction.

(3) The liability of one who is under a public duty to give the information extends to loss suffered by any of the class of persons for whose benefit the duty is created, in any of the transactions in which it is intended to protect them.

15 This traditional approach is still seen in the Engineers Joint Contract Documents Committee Doc. 700, General Conditions for Construction, which states, in section 3.06, "Electronic Data":

A. Unless otherwise stated in the Supplementary Conditions, the data furnished by Owner or Engineer to Contractor, or by Contractor to Owner or Engineer, that may be relied upon are limited to the printed copies (also known as hard copies). Files in electronic media format of text, data, graphics, or other types are furnished only for the convenience of the receiving party.

Any conclusion or information obtained or derived from such electronic files will be at the user's sole risk. If there is a discrepancy between the electronic files and the hard copies, the hard copies govern.

B. Because data stored in electronic media format can deteriorate or be modified inadvertently or otherwise without authorization of the data's creator, the party receiving electronic files agrees that it will perform acceptance tests or procedures within 60 days, after which the receiving party shall be deemed to have accepted the data thus transferred. Any errors detected within the 60-day acceptance period will be corrected by the transferring party.

C. When transferring documents in electronic media format, the transferring party makes no representations as to long term compatibility, usability, or readability of documents resulting from the use of software application packages, operating systems, or computer hardware differing from those used by the data's creator.

In 2007 the American Institute of Architects (AIA) issued the *Digital Data Licensing Agreement*[17] and the *Digital Data Protocol Exhibit*.[18] Rather than limit reliance on digital data, these documents explicitly permit reliance for permitted project purposes.[19] The Associated General Contractors (AGC) similarly adopted more open communication standards with their *Electronic Communications Protocol Addendum*.[20] There are significant differences between the documents: the *Electronic Communications Protocol Addendum* uses a checklist and mechanics approach to data transfer, whereas the *Digital Data Protocol Exhibit* focuses on the procedures, formats, and purposes of the data exchange through the Project Protocol Table.[21] But their differences are dwarfed by their similarities. Both assume that information must be freely transferred and that the receiving party may rely on the information in executing its project responsibilities.

The philosophical shift continued in 2008 when the AGC issued its *Building Information Modeling Addendum*,[22] which was followed shortly thereafter by the AIA's *Building Information Modeling Protocol Exhibit*.[23] Again, the documents differ significantly in focus and methodology,[24] but both seek to structure efficient and enhanced data exchange through the building information model or models. The contractual walls are being torn down and replaced with free-flowing but controlled communications.

16 This is a classic risk management dilemma. Are you better off by isolating yourself from a risk or assuming responsibility for the risk and preventing its occurrence? Contractually limiting risk reduces the exposure—that is, the number of ways you could get sued. Legal risk management generally focuses on reducing exposures. For example, the effect of a loss can be lessened by contractually limiting responsibility. But this may be counterproductive. If the loss occurs, the person disadvantaged by the contractual terms will try to overturn or limit his or her applicability. Litigation becomes an essential tool for enforcing the contractual risk allocation, with significant social and practical costs. But real risk is not the sum of potential exposures; rather, it is the product of loss severity and likelihood of occurrence. Thus, risk can be lessened if the parties work to eliminate or reduce the cause of losses even if, by accepting responsibility, their exposure has increased. This strategy seeks to solve the problem rather than redistribute it. In many instances this will be a more effective strategy, because the most successful battle is one that is never fought.

17 AIA Document C106 (2007).

18 AIA Document E201 (2007).

19 AIA Document E201, sec. 2.4.

20 ConsensusDOCS 200.2 (2007).

21 For a detailed discussion of the ConsensusDOCS and AIA approaches, see, K. Hurtado and H. Ashcraft, *Saving the Trees and Managing the Paper: Developing Meaningful Contract Terms for Construction Project Electronic Communication Protocols* (paper, American Bar Association Forum on the Construction Industry, Chicago, September 2008). The paper is forthcoming in the journal *Construction Lawyer* in 2009.

22 ConsensusDOCS 301 (2008).

23 AIA Document E202 (2008).

24 The *BIM Information Modeling Addendum* uses a more detailed approach to mechanics but a broader brush regarding how the information will be exchanged and used and the level of detail required in the BIM. In contrast, the *Building Information Modeling Protocol Exhibit* uses a very powerful tool, the Model Element Table, to define who is responsible for information, who can use information, and the level of detail of the information on a phase-by-phase basis. The Model Element Table is an extension of the Model Progression Matrix developed by the Technology Committee of the AIA California Council's Integrated Project Delivery Taskforce. See http://www.ipd-ca.net/IPD%20Technology%20Issues.htm.

1.2   The Transformation to Integrated Project Delivery

The development of data exchange and BIM protocols removes barriers to collaborative communication but does not require collaborative action. By themselves, these changes cannot overcome traditional construction practices, such as competitive low bid procurement, guaranteed maximum price, and similar contract structures that have fostered an individualistic, zero-sum approach to construction.[25] Although the AEC industry has praised collaborative behavior, it has used business structures that reward individuals based on their own performance and that foster antagonistic relationships.[26]

Integrated project delivery (IPD) transforms collaboration from a behavior we would like to occur (an aspiration) to a behavior that has consequences (a value). A value is a behavior that is rewarded if achieved and enforced if ignored. Moreover, IPD provides a management and risk-sharing structure that supports a truly collaborative project.

IPD stems from many sources, the most significant being the Project Alliancing initiative developed in the United Kingdom and used most successfully in Australia.[27] The key elements of Project Alliancing are (1) guaranteed payment of participants' direct costs, (2) sharing of project overruns/underruns, (3) joint project management, and (4) waiver of claims between participants. Essentially, once an alliance is formed, the participants are bound to succeed or fail together.

25 These processes, in conjunction with other influences, have resulted in declining labor productivity. According to research by Paul Teicholz at the Stanford University Department of Civil & Environmental Engineering, construction labor productivity declined by approximately 20 percent between 1964 and 2004, whereas industrial productivity increased approximately 200 percent during the same period (P. Teicholz, as reported in "Labor Productivity Declines in the Construction Industry: Causes and Remedies," AECbytes Viewpoint, no. 4, April 14, 2004, and elsewhere). Estimates of waste in construction are similarly alarming. The Construction Industry Institute estimates that 57 percent of all construction activity does not add value. (Construction Industry Institute, 2004, C11) An earlier study concluded that 30 percent of project costs were wasted because of mismanagement caused by the division between design and construction (C. Ibbs et al., Determining the Impact of Various Construction Contract Types and Clauses on Project Performance (Austin TX: Construction Industry Institute Publications 5–1, July, 1986).

26 Consider, for example, a "modern" project delivery approach, such as cost plus/guaranteed maximum price (GMP) contract with preconstruction services and shared cost savings. This is intended to be an efficient project delivery approach that includes contractor expertise through preconstruction costing and constructability reviews and creates an incentive for reducing cost below the GMP target. But the contract structure actually impedes this goal. First, an economically rational contractor should try to avoid cost-saving suggestions during the preconstruction phase. Smart ideas that occur before design is advanced merely lower the GMP, whereas smart ideas that emerge after the GMP is set mean more money in the contractor's pocket. The designer has little incentive to design inexpensively, because there is no financial incentive to do so and runs risks if problems occur during construction. The economically rational architect should design defensively and attempt to transfer responsibility to the contractor. Once construction commences, the situation deteriorates. If an event occurs that might affect project cost, such as an arguable

increase in scope or cost due to an alleged design error, the economically rational contractor must demand a change order to cover these costs. At the time of the event, the contractor cannot know how many additional "events" will occur on this project and whether the total project cost will be within the GMP. Thus, the prudent contractor must claim additional compensation or time, because not doing so means it may have waived its rights to the change and not be able to increase the GMP when it really needs relief. Almost immediately, the project devolves into claims and finger-pointing. Although many projects have been successfully completed using this and other equally noncollaborative project delivery approaches, their success is a testament to the professionalism and selflessness of the participants, not a commendation of the project delivery approach.

27 An excellent introduction to alliancing is the Project Alliancing Practitioners' Guide, Department of Treasury and Finance, State of Victoria, Australia (2006).

In the United States, the Lean Construction Institute began promoting collaborative project structures to support project collaboration. The shift accelerated in 2007 when the AIA's California Council (AIACC) issued its *Integrated Project Delivery: A Working Definition*,[28] which was soon followed by the joint AIA/AIACC *Integrated Project Delivery: A Guide*.[29] AIA also issued a revised policy statement on project delivery, which states:

> The AIA believes that every project delivery process must address the quality, cost-effectiveness, and sustainability of our built environment. This can best be effected through industry-wide adoption of an integrated approach to project delivery methodologies characterized by early involvement of owners, designers, constructors, fabricators and end user/operators in an environment of effective collaboration and open information sharing.[30]

These AIA/AIACC documents provide the theoretical framework for IPD and create a structure whereby the key participants (owner, designers, contractors, and significant trades) are deeply involved from project inception, with information openly shared among them. In addition, the parties share risk and reward based on project outcome, jointly manage the project to achieve shared goals, and agree to limit liability to each other. Although BIM is theoretically not required for IPD, both the *Working Definition* and the *Guide* recognize that BIM is a fundamental collaborative tool and will almost always be used on an integrated project.[31] These fundamental provisions create a value-based virtual organization aligned to the project.

As significant as these structural changes are, IPD requires even more profound changes in belief and behavior. IPD is a trust-based project delivery methodology and will not succeed, regardless of structural changes, unless the team understands why IPD works. For example, these are a few postulates of IPD:

- optimization requires collaboration;
- collaboration unlocks creativity;
- joint control creates joint ownership;

28 See http://ipd-ca.net/IPD%20Definition. htm.

29 See http://www.aia.org/contractdocs/ AIAS077630.

30 AIA Policy Statement 26 (2007). The prior policy statement on project delivery

concluded that many different project delivery methods were acceptable and showed no preference for collaborative processes.

31 "It is understood that integrated project delivery and building information modeling (BIM) are different concepts—the first is a

process and the second a tool. Certainly integrated projects are done without BIM and BIM is used in non-integrated processes. However, the full potential benefits of both IPD and BIM are achieved only when they are used together" (Explanatory Note, *Integrated Project Delivery: A Guide*, 20).

— timely payback on project outcome creates selflessness; and challenge stimulates creativity; but fear creates defensiveness.

Teams need to believe that these assertions are true, and as discussed below, contracts being developed to support IPD must support and embrace the key principles and postulates.

1.3   IPD Contracts as Collaborative Tools

The AGC and AIA have recently issued contract documents that support IPD. However, IPD in the United States is an evolving practice, and experimentation is still the norm. The variance in IPD practice also reflects differences between project teams and between different projects. IPD documents must reflect the participants' differing characteristics, capabilities, and preferences. At a minimum, dimensions such as project duration, project size, the size and financial capability of the participants, type of financing, project complexity, prior IPD experience, and risk tolerance all affect how IPD is implemented. At present, each project needs to be separately crafted, although several different approaches are beginning to emerge.

Multiparty Integrated Agreement
In several recent projects, the author used a contractual approach that translates the Australian Project Alliance into an American commercial and legal framework. Owner, architect, and contractor execute a single multiparty integrated agreement (MPIA) that is consistent with IPD principles and postulates. This contract structure has been used on LEED Platinum tenant improvements and hospital projects, and it is being developed into standard IPD agreements for a national architectural firm and a multidisciplinary program manager. Portions of this approach have also been used on a wide variety of other projects where greater integration is sought, but full integration is not possible because of public procurement restrictions.

Under these contracts, the project team jointly develops financial and other targets based on the owner's program and budget. Using target value design, the team then works collaboratively to design and construct the project to the agreed target. The project is managed by a three-party project management team composed of participant representatives. All project management team decisions must be unanimous, with deadlocks being broken by a majority vote of senior representatives. The owner can still override the nonowner participants, but if an owner's directive, as it is called, is issued, the target cost and schedule will be equitably adjusted. Compensation is based on project outcome, which can result in a nonowner participant's profit being increased, decreased, or even eliminated. The owner guarantees actual costs, however. In addition, the amount of profit can be adjusted based on quality and schedule. Liability is waived between the key parties for damages related to cost and schedule.

ConsensusDOCS 300 Standard Form of Tri-Party Agreement for Collaborative Project Delivery

In 2007 the AGC issued an integrated agreement based on the Lean Construction Institute contract. It expresses a desire for collaboration and imports some concepts of lean construction. Like the MPIA, the owner, contractor, and architect sign a single agreement. Also like the MPIA, the parties share risk and reward based on agreed-upon targets. However, the ConsensusDOCS 300 sets the targets shortly before construction, which removes much of the opportunity for target-based design and much of the incentive for the designer or constructor to develop a cost-efficient approach during the design phase. In addition, because potential savings are found primarily in the construction phase, the designer is placing its profit at risk *after* it has lost control over the outcome. The ConsensusDOCS 300 has options that affect the level of project integration and need to be considered carefully, such as an option to retain traditional liability and risk allocation or to more broadly waive liability. Like all form contracts, the ConsensusDOCS 300 requires modification to tailor it to a specific project, project team, and jurisdiction. It does, however, contain many interesting concepts, and its issuance was an important event in developing IPD in the United States.

American Institute of Architects Integrated Projecy Delivery Agreements

In 2008 the AIA issued two IPD approaches. The first is a transitional set of documents that has separate owner-contractor[32] and owner-architect[33] agreements and a joint set of general conditions.[34] This document series does favor collaboration but does not include the risk sharing, joint project control, or liability waivers that full integration requires. The second approach is fully integrated but more complex and requires extensive customization for specific projects and specific jurisdictions. The AIA's Single Purpose Entity (SPE) Agreement for Integrated Project Delivery[35]

32 AIA Document A195.   33 AIA Document B195.   34 AIA Document A295.

implements IPD by using a separate limited liability company jointly owned by the owner, contractor, and architect. The owner contracts with this single purpose entity to design and construct the project. The SPE manages the project though a controlling board in which the owner has a majority interest. The SPE contracts with the architect and contractor on a cost or reduced-profit basis, with final profitability based on project outcome. The SPE approach is significantly more complex than other forms and requires consideration of licensing, taxation, and corporate compliance issues that the others do not require. Because of the legal complexity of this approach, it will most likely be used on larger projects. The SPE approach is appropriate for some project types, however, and many of the document's concepts can be used with other approaches.

1.4   Legal Implications of Collaboration[36]

Collaboration changes the rules, and whether these changes are threatening or refreshing depends on your point of view. For example, if information is freely exchanged with the intent that it be used and relied on, then concepts of privity and the economic-loss doctrine are largely obsolete. Designers in particular are concerned that they are now exposed to a broader range of potential claimants, including contractors and subcontractors. But collaboration can also serve to reduce potential liability, as shown by a narrowing of the hallowed Spearin doctrine.

Introduced by the Supreme Court in 1918, the Spearin doctrine allocates design risk by implying an owner's warranty that plans are complete and accurate. The Spearin court found that "the one who provides the plans and specification for a construction project warrants that those plans and specifications are free from defect."[37] Although initially a defensive doctrine, Spearin has evolved into an offensive weapon that permits contractors to recover damages whenever plans have errors or omissions.[38] In principle, Spearin does not affect design professionals, because the implied warranty flows from owner to contractor. In practice, however, it overshadows much of construction litigation because it encourages the contractor to allege design deficiencies that trigger the absolute Spearin warranty and forces the owner to assert indemnity claims against its designer.

35 AIA Document C195.

36 The issues discussed are a sampling of new issues raised by collaboration. For additional discussion of legal issues in

BIM-enabled collaborative projects, see H. Ashcraft, "Building Information Modeling."

37 United States v. Spearin, 248 U.S. 132 (1918).

38 See, e.g., Hercules Inc. v. United States, 24 F.3d 188 (1994), 197.

But if the contractor participates in design development, can it rely on Spearin? Decisions involving performance[39] specifications strongly suggest that Spearin is less effective in a collaborative environment because there is no need to imply a warranty to design information provided by the contractor.[40] The applicability of Spearin to hybrid specifications—those that blend prescriptive and performance requirements—has also been questioned.[41] Spearin will not apply. In a fully modeled project, particularly in a collaborative project where subcontractor and vendor information is incorporated into the design, it appears that courts would turn to cases of hybrid specifications to determine whether to imply a warranty. This will be a factual inquiry, but the deeper a contractor's involvement in the design, the less likely a warranty will be implied. And as recently noted, "It is not unreasonable to project that the threshold for invocation of Spearin by a contractor and BIM participant…will be set quite high."[42]

Collaboration also impinges on professional responsibility rules that were created for an insular world. The tripartite division between design, construction, and ownership places the architect and engineer as masters of the design and, consequently, as the parties responsible for protecting the public against unsafe structures. To achieve this public policy, the appropriate design professional must sign and seal the construction documents to signify responsibility for the design. Moreover, the statutes and regulations require the designer to be "in responsible charge,"[43] which requires that work be performed by the licensed professional or under his or her supervision. But in a collaborative, BIM-enabled project, a gray area exists at the intersection of work performed by the design professional, work performed by the software, and work performed by unlicensed professionals.

Intelligent modeling software can perform certain design work historically performed by design professionals. Structural design and detailing software, for example, is capable of modifying the connection details in response to design changes, such as the length of a beam. This occurs without input from the design professional and in response to an algorithm that the design professional did not develop and may not even understand. In

39 The Spearin doctrine does not apply to performance specifications (because the contractor is not being told how to accomplish the result) unless the desired outcome is impossible to achieve or, in some jurisdictions, commercially impracticable.

40 Austin Co. V. United States, 314 F.2d at 520.

41 H. Hammersmith and E. Lozowick, "Can the Spearin Doctrine Survive in a Design-Build World: Who Bears the Responsibility for Hybrid Specifications?" American College of Construction Lawyers Journal 2, no. 1 (winter 2008); Ashcraft, "Building Information Modeling," 7.

42 T. O'Brien, "Successfully Navigating Your Way through the Electronically Managed Project," Construction Lawyer 28, no. 3 (summer 2008): 31–32. O'Brien

also concludes that the Spearin warranty is weakened in collaborative projects.

43 In California, for example, architects must be in "responsible control" (California Business and Professions Code, sec. 5531.5) and engineers must be in "responsible charge" (California Business and Professions Code, sec. 6703). These requirements reverberate through many other statutes and regulations.

addition, the ability to exchange data between models, and to collaborate through the models, creates the possible—and likely desirable—result that design details created by subcontractors and vendors will be incorporated into the model and the final construction documents.[44]

These issues are not entirely new. For years, engineers have relied on analysis programs using programming code the engineers have never seen and might not be able to understand.[45] Similarly, some portion of design has always existed in the coordination drawings, shop drawings, and submittals issued by the contractor and its subcontractors. But what had been ancillary or supporting documents are now, with BIM, part of the model, and possibly the contract documents themselves. The gap between statutory requirements and good professional practice is widening. Statutory definitions of responsible charge are out of step with emerging practice and must be modified to support design collaboration while preserving public safety and confidence.[46]

Finally, BIM affects the standard of care at several levels. At the most basic level, is it below the standard of care *not* to use BIM if using BIM can readily solve design issues that resist solution when attacked with traditional tools? Clash detection of complex structures is an obvious example. Historically, designs were developed to an advanced state with some details intentionally omitted to be completed by the contractor from the final but for some systems still "diagrammatic," design. In part, this practice was justified because the designer did not know which specific systems would be chosen by the contractor. In other cases, the final layouts were deemed part of the contractor's means and methods and, therefore, not the designer's concern. More often than one would like, this resulted in designs that could not be coordinated by the contractor or, if they could eventually be coordinated, had a layout that was inefficient and expensive. Many delay and impact claims are born from this coordination problem.

BIM almost eliminates coordination problems because it allows the designer, the contractor, and the subcontractors to dimensionally check their respective work. Physical conflict issues can be resolved during the design phase and confirmed with

---

44 This recently occurred in a Northern California hospital where the final mechanical drawings were prepared by the mechanical subcontractor but stamped by the mechanical engineer (who had worked collaboratively with the subcontractor and could be said to be in responsible charge).

45 In the early days of the author's litigation practice, engineers would occasionally be required to produce the programming

code used to analyze an engineering problem and, before introducing the results, explain to a confused court and jury how the program was constructed and why it was reliable. This requirement has largely evaporated as analysis software has become commonplace.

46 On October 31, 2008, a National Council of Architectural Registration Boards (NCARB) task force held hearings regarding

professional responsibility in collaborative environments and has recommended modifications to NCARB's *Legislative Guidelines and Model Law* for board consideration in June 2009 (NCARB press release, January 29, 2009).

electronic submittals. Given the expense and disruption caused by clashes discovered during construction, and the ease with which this problem is solved, does the standard of care *require* that the designer use tools that eliminate this costly problem? In the author's opinion, traditionally coordinated 2-D drawings are no longer sufficient for complex structures, particularly those with significant mechanical, electrical, and plumbing systems.[47]

There are also standard of care issues arising from *how* BIM is implemented. Although it is convenient to discuss *the* model used for a project, in practice, project design is an amalgamation of interlocking models created by different project participants. These federated models must be able to exchange information accurately, which requires forethought and discussion between participants. In addition, the designer needs to determine the model's granularity—that is, the detail to which information is depicted as this affects the interface between the designer's and the implementer's responsibilities. Similarly, the designer needs to determine what information will reside in the model and what information will reside in specifications or 2-D CADD drawings. Finally, the process of collaboration raises questions regarding who owns the model or other collaborative work. As a general rule, the creator of intellectual property owns it. But if two or more parties contribute[48] to the intellectual property, it becomes a joint work owned by all of them. In a BIM-enabled collaborative project, ownership rights must be appropriately allocated by contract.

Using BIM to solve increasingly complex and sophisticated problems will naturally lead to its use in collaborative settings. Deeper collaboration will expose the limitations of current business and contractual structures and lead to exploration of project delivery methods aligned with collaboration, such as IPD. And IPD, which involves communication and collaboration between multiple participants, needs a common language and communication platform, which leads back to BIM. This reinforcing evolution requires development of project and contractual structures that intelligently allocate risk, reward, and control and also enhance efficiency, quality, and sustainability. Although the ultimate solution is not yet in sight, the journey has begun.

---

47 The author represented the owner of a university laboratory where a partially diagrammatic design was used for the mechanical, electrical, and plumbing systems. When the systems were modeled, many conflicts were found, supporting the contractor's argument that it had to "redesign" the systems, not merely coordinate them.

48 The contribution must be more than just offering ideas or editing. Part of the joint work must have been created by the person claiming ownership. However, the author is aware of a project where the contractor and the architect each worked in the same digital model providing content that was embedded in the model. Absent contract language granting title to the owner, both would have had ownership rights to the BIM.

Overcoming Embedded Inefficiencies

Rodd W. Merchant

The inefficiencies of the building design and construction industry are well documented. Equally well chronicled are the potential productivity and economic benefits that today's readily available technology solutions offer. Despite clear, demonstrated opportunities, however, global adoption and integration of technology by the architecture, engineering, and construction (AEC) industry remains pragmatically slow.

Industry fragmentation, lack of interoperability, and hardened business practices are often cited as reasons for the failure of the AEC industry to capitalize on the benefits of automation. Technology alone cannot force process change, but it has the potential to enable it. However, evolution is inevitable. Global economic competition and a growing awareness of the importance of sustainable resource consumption are applying new pressures and demanding change across the AEC supply chain. Architects, engineers, and builders now realize that the horizontal alignment of technology and process-driven design will transform building and component design and construction. Forward-thinking firms are taking advantage of recent advancements in technology and redefining their contracts and organizational structures. It further suggests that early successes realized through technology automation will irrevocably reshape the art, science, and organization of architecture and design.

Process improvement through automation in automobile, aircraft, and other manufacturing industries occurred rapidly through the 1980s and 1990s, with model-based virtual design and assembly offering the ability to predict and resolve costly system conflicts before the assembly stage. In nearly all manufacturing and process-related businesses except the building industry, the benefits of virtual assembly and system integration are so important that they have become commonplace. Stanford University's Center for Integrated Facility Engineering has illustrated that the building industry's failure to capitalize on the benefits offered by technology has resulted in a decrease in productivity over this same period of time.[1]

In construction, the lack of interoperability standards allowing for the meaningful exchange of building information data is often cited as the primary reason for the failure to automate. Although important, interoperability alone will not facilitate technology adoption. Electronic data interchange (EDI) has improved over time, yet the number of firms actually using EDI remains small. The underlying causes are not technological but structural. Today

1   CIFE research indicates that over a thirty-four year perior, productivity of U.S. construction has declined slightly while productivity of all other non-farm industries has more than doubled. For more information visit http://cife.stanford.edu.

nearly all methods of building project delivery are structured, legally and otherwise, to sever the interrelated functions of design, material procurement, handling, fabrication, shipping, installation, and operation. Current model contracts are purposefully structured to limit the risk and exposure of each player in the process, which in effect, detracts from the completed work at the owner's expense. As a result, participants tend to work in silos focused solely on their assigned scope, ignoring the interrelated activities of others. Furthermore, the legal and insurance systems offer little assistance to those who wish to pursue alternative forms of project delivery. So in the absence of current case law, fear of the unknown holds automation hostage. In order for global adoption of model-based technology to occur, the industry must restructure the current transactional business process models and develop practical strategies for the exchange of electronic design data.[2] In his essay, cited below, attorney Christopher Nobel explains how alternative delivery models such as Project Alliance redefine the relationship between the owner, key designers, and key general and trade contractors into a single "relational based" contract that rewards alliance members for behaviors that benefit the project.[3]

It is important to note that designers adopting new technologies geared toward automation and efficiency tend to bear a disproportionate amount of the cost relative to the benefits they receive. The costs associated with creating solid models are largely born by architects and engineers. The real value of data-rich models produced during the design process tends to be realized downstream, during fabrication, construction, and building operation. There is also an increasing awareness that the building industry must become a more intelligent consumer of finite natural resources, which drives interest in more intelligent and automated design. The sustainability movement has gained considerable momentum of late and is now attracting the attention of building owners and developers. This bodes well for technology since automation facilitates many of the objectives embodied by green building, such as reduced waste, off-site fabrication, and advanced energy studies.

In their book *Refabricating Architecture*, Stephen Kieran and James Timberlake explore how architects, by relinquishing responsibility for construction means, methods, and sequences of assembly to the builder, have allowed the compromise of building form (thought to be their exclusive purview).[4] Over the last twenty-

2   P. Bernstein and J. Pittman, "Barriers to the Adoption of Building Information Modeling in the Building Industry" (white paper, Autodesk, Waltham, MA, 2004).

3   C. L. Noble, "Adapting the Project Alliance Delivery System to the U.S. Legal and Construction Environment" (paper presented at the Construction SuperConference, December 2000).

4   S. Kieran and J. Timberlake, *Refabricating Architecture: How Manufacturing Methodologies Are Poised to Transform Building Construction* (New York: McGraw-Hill, 2004), xi–xiii, 2–14.

five years, building systems have become increasingly complex: the information age has brought an explosion of product options and specialized systems for everything from exterior cladding to computer-controlled HVAC. It is impossible for today's architect to be an expert in the myriad air distribution, piping, electrical, communication, and security systems, just to name a few. The design of these systems involves highly specialized engineering analysis, and one can quickly understand that orchestrating these systems into a completed building is a monumental task.

Those in construction practice note an alarming trend in project management by junior-level architectural staff who lack the in-the-trenches experience required to effectively manage the design and coordination of increasingly complex building structures and systems. Architectural documents from which contractors must build are often incomplete and uncoordinated. This decline has inspired a shift in the strategy and organization of the construction industry, with builders often either hiring in-house staff or retaining outside professional consultants to work through complex interface and coordination issues.

The American Institute of Steel Construction (AISC) was an early proponent of technological integration and process improvement. This organization of structural engineers, fabricators, detailers, and erectors supported the development of the CIMSteel Integration Standards/Version 2 (CIS/2), which utilizes a neutral file format to achieve interoperability between design, detailing, and fabrication programs, effectively bridging the disconnect between previously incompatible systems, such as structural analysis and design, detailing, procurement and processing, and CNC fabrication.[5]

Integration standards such as CIS/2 have been successful in exchanging product data, but complete integration requires exchange of process information, such as resource, sequence, and logistical requirements. Current research suggests that additional object extensions are necessary to handle process-driven events.[6] In time, complete data structures incorporating process descriptions may exist, but even today engineers and builders can extract value from virtual building models and assemblies. In fact, those extracting the greatest value from virtual building models are subcontractors who fabricate and install a specific building component or system, such as the steel frame superstructure.

5   G. S. Coleman and J. W. Jun, "Interoperability and the Construction Process: A White Paper for Building Owners and Project Decision-Makers," http://www.construction.org/clientuploads/resource_center/facilities_mamagement/

InteroperabilityandtheBuilding Process.pdf.

6   M. Danso-Amoako, W. O'Brien, and R. Issa, "A Case Study of IFC and CIS/2 Support for Steel Supply Chain

Processes," (paper presented at the Tenth International Conference on Computing in Civil and Building Engineering [ICCCBE-10], Weimar, Germany, June 2–4, 2004; published in conference proceedings).

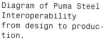

Diagram of Puma Steel
Interoperability
from design to produc-
tion.

Puma Steel - Interoperability

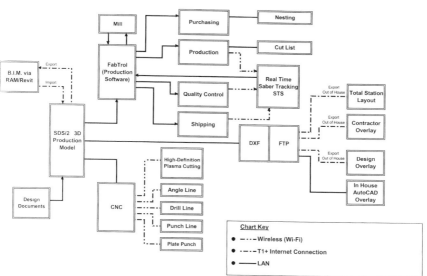

CIS/2 is the beginning of the integration process in the steel industry, but in order for the benefits of automation to be realized, the traditional project delivery model must be reorganized to completely align and integrate the activities of design, procurement, fabrication, and installation. Conceiving of the structural steel frame for a building using the traditional contract model of design-bid-build severs the design from the critical activities of purchasing, detailing, fabricating, shipping, and erecting. In this approach, the engineer generally completes the design before the award of the steel subcontract. Not knowing who will win the contract, the engineer cannot incorporate critical information such as material pricing and availability, equipment capability, connection preferences (welded versus bolted), prefabrication opportunities, shipping limitations, and so on, all of which could, and most likely should, influence the design. The resulting inefficiencies cost the project (and owner) considerable time and money.

One possible model for restructuring the steel subcontract allows the frame design to incorporate downstream activities, such as material availability, shop capacity, shipping restrictions, material staging, production rates, and erection preferences. EDI and interoperability are not the most important factors, but rather key ingredients enabling the team to eliminate duplicate effort and to speed delivery.

Under this design-build/strategic-alliance model, the fabricator still holds the prime contract for the steel frame, but the engineering is provided under subcontract to the fabricator. For this model to work, the steel subcontract must be awarded early on, allowing participation and input by all team members. Since the engineering is provided by the fabricator, the preferences of the detailer, mill provider, erector, and other product suppliers can be incorporated into the design. The team internally controls activities such as coordination, schedule milestones, and submittal and shop drawing processes. During construction, the team also handles any problems arising from fit-up or fabrication errors, eliminating the need for requests for information or nonconformance requests on the part of the general contractor and/or architect. A true partnership forms, because all team members are financially tied to the success of their partners. Profits (or losses) are shared by all at project completion through a predetermined percentage allocation. As an integral part of the design team, the steel frame engineer is involved throughout the design process, coordinating the frame with the building's architecture and manufacturing extension partnership (MEP) systems. The result is a custom steel frame, designed, fabricated, and installed through a process more closely resembling that of manufacturing.

Rodd Merchant,
design-build/strategic-
alliance model

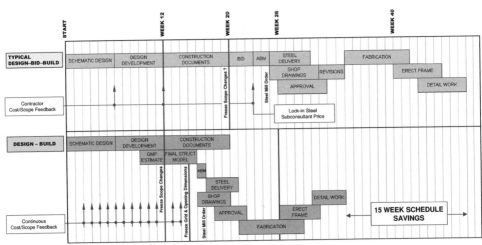

Typical 700 Ton Office Building

As demonstrated in the steel frame example, automation can greatly enhance alignment of analysis and design activities with detailing, procurement, fabrication, and erection. Utilizing CIS/2, frame data is passed from engineer to fabricator.[7] A detailed look at process control in the fabricator's shop further underscores the significance of software interoperability. Each time the original data is used to control a downstream activity it becomes more valuable, because the time and effort required to recreate the data is eliminated.

The benefits of horizontal process alignment and automation are best demonstrated through a schedule comparison with traditional design-bid-build delivery. For a typical 700-ton office building, design-build delivery offers a potential fifteen-week (30 percent) schedule reduction compared with traditional delivery. The impact on the total project is significant, since erection of the structural frame is a critical path activity. Downstream activities such as the installation of exterior walls, glazing, roofing, and MEP systems cannot begin until the structural frame is in place, and so speeding project delivery has the benefit not only of saving the owner money during construction but also of allowing the owner to begin generating revenue sooner.

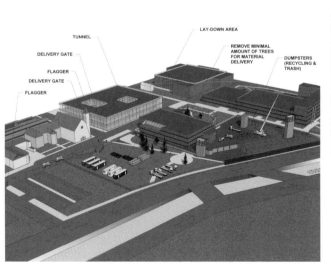

Rendering of JE Dunn steel construction.

<

JE Dunn construction, rendering of site workflow.

7   R. Merchant, J. Petersen, and W. Lewis. "Process Improvement through Interoperability and Teamwork" (paper presented at the American Institute of Steel Construction: North American Steel Construction Conference, February 2006).

JE Dunn construction, window rendering and detail
drawings for installation sequence

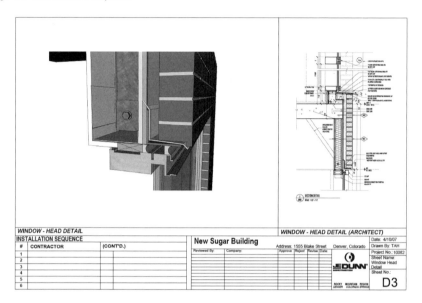

Wall sequence drawings

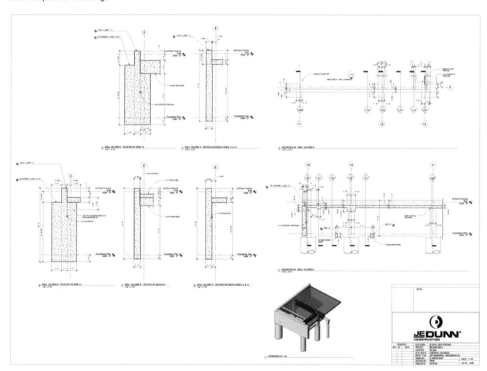

In addition to significant schedule savings, a number of other benefits result from a team approach. A common point of friction between designers and contractors is so-called value engineering, the process of reducing project cost while attempting to maintain performance and quality. Oftentimes the contractor or subcontractor suggests cost- or schedule-saving alternatives after the engineer's design is complete. Without the promise of additional compensation, most designers resist making changes to their already-completed documents. Under the integrated design-build model, however, the subcontractor implements a continuous system of cost and scope feedback early in the design process. This allows the architect and other subconsultants to incorporate cost- and schedule-saving ideas into their documents at the appropriate moment in the design process.

Yet another benefit is the ability to eliminate or greatly reduce price instability. A steel mill order, for example, can be placed several weeks earlier than in the traditional process. Early procurement can help soften material price escalation that often adversely affects project budgets. Including a mill partner as part of the team can further control costs through alignment of member sizing with inventory on hand in the supply yard, thus eliminating schedule delays for long-lead or special roll items.

The potential schedule savings that design-build delivery offers for individual building components is compelling. Reducing the construction schedule of even a moderate-sized project can save as much as $100,000. Savvy building owners such as General Motors have found that virtual assembly coupled with alignment of design and construction activities results in capital projects that are delivered faster, more inexpensively, and with superior quality than by traditional delivery methods.[8] More and more component suppliers are discovering that aligning engineering and design with fabrication and installation offers the ability to maximize their capabilities as well as those of their team members. Products are fabricated to tighter tolerances, with less material waste, and delivered and installed in less time than with traditional delivery methods.

The popularity of performance-based or prescriptive design specifications has steadily increased. Ever-increasing numbers of product suppliers and trade organizations are recommending their use for components including curtain walls, metal floor and roof decking, metal bar joists, wood trusses, steel stairs, and precast

8   T. Sayer, "Soaring into the Virtual World: Build It First Digitally," *Engineering News-Record (ENR)*, October 10, 2005; T. Sayer, "Digital Modeling: Early Adopters Find the Best Models Are Digital Virtuosos," *Engineering News-Record (ENR)*, October 2, 2006.

concrete. A recent newcomer to performance-based specifications is the American Concrete Institute, with regard to ready-mixed concrete. As adoption of component design-build and BIM technology increases, the number of organizations promoting performance-based specifications is likely to increase.

Just as component suppliers are beginning to see the benefits of horizontal process integration, engineers, in turn, are finding new business opportunities in working with subcontractors and suppliers. These new business opportunities not only restructure contractual relationships but offer the engineer willing to step outside the arena of traditional consulting services the opportunity to command higher fees. Producing electronic design data that is dimensionally suitable for fabrication is generally beyond the traditional standard of care in the AEC industry: architects and engineers are not required to produce drawings that are 100 percent dimensionally accurate. Subcontractors and builders, on the other hand, recognize the importance of digital accuracy and are generally willing to compensate creators for their efforts. As a result, design professionals working in a design-build environment, compensated for higher-precision design deliverables, often report that their fees for such projects are higher than with traditional design-bid-build delivery. Further, the effort required to resolve issues during the construction administration phase of the project is reduced by means of better coordination, fewer field errors, and a diminished number of contractor-requested alternatives.

Regardless of delivery method, the entity most responsible for procuring, coordinating, and delivering the project remains the general contractor (GC). As projects increase in complexity, the diminished role of the design architect has resulted in a disproportionate increase in responsibilities for the builder. It is the GC who generally establishes the project budget and determines site logistic and sequencing requirements. The cost impact of these critical activities has prompted more and more building owners and developers to engage the GC early, during concept or schematic design, since it is the GC who is most in tune with market costs and labor conditions. As a result of this expanded role, many builders have changed their organizational structure to include in-house designers, architects, and engineers working to align a building's form and function with the logistical and scheduling challenges of construction. For example, in the area of risk management, contractors routinely utilize professional peer review by internal design professionals and have adopted BIM to plan logistics and sequencing and elevate field workforce knowledge. Often, GCs hire architects as in-house staff to create these models.

The use of BIM by contractors and subcontractors undoubtedly will increase over the next decade. Early adopters have demonstrated that the benefits of technology integration far outweigh the associated risks. The construction community's primary trade organization, the Associated General Contractors of America, actively promotes the use of BIM.[9] As more and more builders adopt technology, they will simultaneously look to capitalize on their investment by restructuring their contractual agreements to take advantage of horizontal process integration. This transformation will open the door for architects and engineers to redefine their roles and relationships, and enable positive change in an otherwise stagnant industry. As component-based design flourishes, the result may be an unbundling of traditional design and consulting services. That is, consultants traditionally administered under the architect's prime contract, such as engineers, may shift to being under the auspices of the construction manager or a subcontractors.

9   See *The Contractor's Guide to Building Information Modeling—BIM*, Associated General Contractors of America, 2006.

Controlling Intellectual Property
Christopher Noble

"Who will own the model?" This is a question that often arises in discussions of building information modeling (BIM). Those who jump right in to offer an opinion can get stuck very quickly, and for a number of good reasons. One is the tendency for design professionals, and for us, their legal advisers, to apply intellectual property concepts in a primitive and imprecise manner to this issue. This has clouded our understanding of the rights of ownership, reproduction, and use of traditional design documentation and thus made it very difficult to apply these concepts in a direct and rational manner to BIM and other digital files. Another reason is our failure to look beyond our limited areas of activity and expertise and learn from those who are engaged in other creative and professional endeavors. We must try to overcome both of these limitations as we begin to address the question of BIM ownership.

Historically, most design contracts have focused on legal ownership of pieces of paper produced by the design professionals, commonly referred to as "instruments of service." They have distinguished between "original" documents and "copies" of documents. Contracts drafted by owners typically provided that all originals and all copies were the "property of the owner" and had to be delivered to the owner when the contract was completed or terminated. The forms of contract drafted by the American Institute of Architects (AIA) normally stated that the originals were the property of the architect and that the owner was permitted to keep copies unless the contract with the architect was terminated, in which case the owner had to return the copies to the architect and/or refrain from using them to complete or modify the project.

Ownership of tangible documents does not carry with it the right to make copies of the documents or to develop the documents further into more refined or derivative forms. These rights are governed not by the law of sales but by the United States Copyright Act (Title 17 of the *United States Code*). The holder of the copyright has the legal power to permit or license authorized copying and to forbid or obtain damages for unauthorized copying.

Until 1990 the concept of copyright only applied to the drawings and specifications: it did not apply to actual constructed buildings, which anyone could measure, photograph, and thereby replicate on another site (even virtually next door, as was the case in a well-known court decision involving two New York–area McMansions). In 1990 the Copyright Act was amended to make *buildings* copyrightable as "architectural works." In the years since this statute passed, there have been a number of important judicial decisions dealing with its enforcement. In the same period of time, one would have expected owner-architect agreements and other industry contracts to address the issues raised by the copyrightability of buildings, but contracts almost never address them, since they are still focused on who owns and can use the originals and copies of paper drawings, specifications, and other instruments of service.

The copyright is initially held by the "author" of the work in question. As recently as 1987 the standard AIA owner-architect agreement form stated that the architect was deemed to be the author of all the instruments of service. In 1997 the AIA changed its standard forms to refer to the architect and its consultants as the authors of their respective instruments of service. This change recognized that there are likely to be many contributors to a set of drawings and specifications. However, it assumed that their contributions could be separated into discrete instruments. There are no commonly used contract clauses that define or describe "authorship" of jointly produced drawings, of construction documents produced by architects of record on the basis of design architects' preliminary drawings, or of details drawn by drafting services located in India or elsewhere.

And what about that other instrument of service, the project manual? The various sections of text may have been provided by an independent specification writer, by the AIA, MasterSpec, or some other standard document source, or by manufacturers who publish proprietary specification sections relating to their products. Finally, an increasing number of projects contain components or systems that are designed by engineers engaged or employed by contractors or subcontractors (such as curtain wall fabricators) in accordance with performance specifications produced by the design team under "design delegation." These are not included among the instruments of service governed by architectural contracts, and construction contracts have traditionally been silent on the ownership of and copyright in drawings and other documents produced by the contractor or its subcontractors.

From this brief description of the predigital world, it can be seen that the issues of authorship and copyright have not been clearly identified, much less addressed. It follows that we should have appropriately modest expectations about how quickly and competently the design professions and construction industry will address the issues of intellectual property rights in the digital databases that, taken together, will constitute the building information model for any given project. It is going to take a while to figure this out, and it is going to take even longer to apply it in an intelligent way to a large number of projects and situations.

It is clear that the Copyright Act will continue to provide the relevant legal authority for analyzing the rights of the various contributors to and users of the database. However, we who advise design and construction professionals will have to achieve a more detailed and sophisticated understanding of how the act applies to our industry. For instance, one of the legal doctrines that we should have resolved in the paper world but did not is the concept of a joint work. Section 101 of the Copyright Act defines a joint work as "a work prepared by two or more authors with the intention that their contributions be merged into inseparable or interdependent parts of a unitary whole." Section 201 of the Copyright Act states, "The authors of a joint work are co-owners of copyright in the work." Taken together, these two provisions mean that unless each author's contribution is distinct, discrete, and separately distinguishable within the collaborative work, the intention of the authors must be examined. Did they intend to retain a separate copyright in their own contributions, or did they intend to have their contributions merged into a joint work in which they share the copyright and all the rights and benefits arising out of it?

In the paper world, we did not clearly analyze the question of whether or not portions of the instruments of service prepared by different architects, engineers, and consultants constitute "inseparable or interdependent parts of a unitary whole." As noted above, recent AIA contract forms have stated that the architect and its consultants "shall be deemed the authors and owners of their respective Instruments of Service and shall retain all common law, statutory and other reserved rights, including copyrights." A clause such as this is evidence that, for instance, the architect holds the copyright in the "A" drawings in a contract set and that the electrical engineer owns the copyright in the "E" drawings. But the "E" drawings may have been produced on base sheets provided by the architect, to which information relating to the electrical system was added by the electrical engineer. Whose instruments of service are these sheets, to which both design professionals contributed information and graphic content? Similarly, in the many projects for which a design architect has taken the architectural design process through the design development phase, and the architect of record has produced more detailed construction documents for issuance to the contractor, who can say that these construction documents are not a joint work of the design architect and the architect of record? (And, significantly, who can remember drafting or reading a design contract that clearly defined the documents as a joint work and allocated the rights of the two designers accordingly?)

And what of the now-copyrightable building itself? Is it a joint work of all the design consultants who contributed to it, or are their contributions, if copyrightable at all, subject to their separate individual copyrights?

If we study the application of the joint work concept to predigital documents and architectural works, we will exercise our analytical muscles in a way that will help us to examine how the concept might apply to building information models and other collaboratively developed digital files.

As already noted, there are many areas of creative endeavor that can teach design and construction professionals about applicable copyright and intellectual property concepts that they have ignored in the past. For instance, it takes a number of skills and contributions to make a traditional comic book: those of a writer, a penciler, an inker, and a colorist. Recently, a writer who put words in the mouths of some of the characters in a wildly successful series of comic books claimed that he was a joint owner of the copyright of the characters themselves and thus was entitled to a portion of the royalties derived from the characters' appearance in derivative works, such as movies and video games. After undertaking an extensive analysis of "joint works" and related concepts, an appellate court confirmed that he was so entitled.

There are dozens and dozens of similar court decisions in areas that do not, at first, seem to be related to architecture and construction but that are in fact relevant to the interpretation of the Copyright Act as it applies to these fields. We who advise design and construction professionals will be both challenged and enriched as we expand our knowledge of copyright provisions beyond those that apply to paper documents and constructed buildings, into areas that are new to us but are well known in the worlds of software development and marketing, e-commerce, and the entertainment industry. In this effort we will have as much to learn from Google as from Gehry, but in our race to address the issues presented by the new technology, we must not forget to undertake the analysis we neglected to do in the paper world.

In the future, contracts and licensing agreements will be more important than ever. Written contracts play a greater role in design and construction than in almost any other industry, in part because our industry consists of many independent participants who come together on a project-by-project basis rather than of large integrated entities with stable, continuing relationships. In any given project, the participants make most of their own rules by contract, instead of relying on the default positions provided by statutes and other governing laws such as, for instance, the Copyright Act.

The problem with the current situation is that the various contracts between and among the project participants are usually inconsistent and uncoordinated with respect to many things, including intellectual property rights. The architect often purports to convey rights to the owner that he has not acquired from his engineering and other consultants (perhaps because the architect's project manager, whose job it is to get the consultant contracts signed, has dropped the ball and moved on to more seemingly pressing tasks). The construction contract may be negotiated by an owner's lawyer who was not on board when the owner signed the owner-architect agreement, which the lawyer has not read. The contractor has a standard form of subcontract that he uses on every project and that bears no relationship to the various prime contracts he signs with owners, except for a generic and unclear "flowdown" clause that is likely to create as much confusion as it avoids.

This cacophony of contracts has not been a disaster with respect to intellectual property rights in our industry, because so little has been at stake. Architects, for instance, have traditionally been more concerned with avoiding liability for unauthorized use of their drawings than with obtaining compensation for such use. But, when the value of digital information can be leveraged over the life cycle of single and multiple projects, and when that information can generate valuable efficiencies in the design and construction of the project for which it is created, what is at stake can be multiplied exponentially. Neither the Copyright Act, taken alone, nor the industry's primitive and inefficient project contracting procedures are up to the job of capturing, allocating, and harvesting that value.

There is no one simple answer to this problem, but there are several possible approaches to solving it. In some cases, very strong and well-organized owners, contractors, project managers, and architects can create fully integrated contractual systems that deal effectively with intellectual property rights and take the lead in negotiating them with other project stakeholders. In some other cases, innovative project delivery methods can incorporate intellectual property principles that are consistent with shared commercial and liability risks and rewards. At this writing there are a number of initiatives under way to develop single, projectwide contract forms to effectuate such new methods, often referred to under the rubric of integrated project delivery. Some of these initiatives are based on the "Project Alliance" delivery system developed and utilized successfully in the United Kingdom, Canada, and Australia. Others are based on collaborative contracts developed by Sutter Health Care, the Lean Construction Institute, and the architectural firm NBBJ. The AIA and the Consensus-Docs group headed by the Associated General Contractors of America are expected to issue integrated contract forms such as these in the near future.

There may be another untapped opportunity to rationalize not only intellectual property rights but also commercial and liability contract terms. Over the last decade, commercially available project extranets have become more stable, robust, reliable, useful, and economical. They are used to some extent in most major projects in this country but are still process tools, not content tools. In the future, they could, however, be populated with content, becoming vehicles for the rationalization and coordination of intellectual property. In that case, certain contract terms would likely be applicable to all the project participants who utilize the extranet, with design professionals, consultants, contractors, or suppliers passing through a number of contractual screens before being given access to the project information database. These screens could be as automatic as the click-through licenses that we all accept when we upgrade our software, or they could be interactive expert systems through which detailed contracts are negotiated and drafted online, under programmed constraints that insure compatibility with other project contracts. The operative question is who would control this contractual content: software developers, facilities managers, contractors, lawyers, claims consultants (now serving as program managers), or industry associations? The possibilities are endless, and the implications are significant.

We have come full circle on the question, "Who will own the model?" by asking, "Who will control the allocation of intellectual property rights in extranet-based contractual access procedures?" Along the way, we have identified the Copyright Act as the primary source of rules and guidelines, which we should seek to understand and apply in a more sophisticated manner than we have in the past. By expanding our field of vision to include the experience of other industries, professions, and collaborative creative endeavors, which will be increasingly relevant to the design professions and the construction industry, we will enter into a new digital age with confidence in our control of the building information model.

Marketing and Positioning Design
Phillip G. Bernstein

The increasing use of digital design and manufacturing method-ologies is changing both the means of production and architects' access to the marketplace of building, particularly in the creation of housing. Attempts to leverage the aesthetic, performance, and production advantages of computer-based techniques can be found at every point in the continuum of the housing market, from "bespoke" custom homes designed by individual architects to lower-costto standardized housing created by "production" home builders. Thus, this market provides a useful platform for exploring how these methods have changed the roles and relationships of designers, constructors, and consumers in the building industry and for examining the role of the architect, the design-to-produc-tion process, and the implications for both market reach and the quality of the results.

It is generally understood that fewer than ten percent of buildings constructed in modern, market-based economies are designed by architects, meaning that a vast majority of the built environment has been created by means other than the dysfunc-tional opposition of architect as advocate of design and contractor as defender of practicality. This dichotomy is particularly marked in the design and construction of houses, where many young archi-tects have established their careers and explored their ideas with individual—and, typically, very wealthy—clients. Yet the vast major-ity of houses built in the modern age are the products of large production builders who are responsible for building hundreds of thousands of "units" yearly. Architectural intervention—and, many might argue, good design—is rarely if ever apparent in the results, which are driven, like all consumer products, by the specific and detailed demands of the mass marketplace.

In the residential market, as in other arenas within the indus-try, the means of conceiving and producing construction is being transformed by the incorporation of digital representation and computer-controlled manufacturing techniques. There is growing interest among architects in exploiting both the expressive power of these tools and their potential to put architect-designed build-ings within reach of a wider market. If the use of digital modeling tools can more efficiently drive the computer-controlled processes of fabrication and assembly, the argument goes, more of the archi-tect's design ideas might be built and quality design will become available to a bigger target market of customers.

Yet even the use of the term *customer* is anathema to a traditional practitioner and signals the inherent tension in the opportunity. It evokes an image of a consumer merely receiving a product created at arm's length by a manufacturer who determines the characteristics of that product without direct interaction with

the final buyer. Producers of manufactured housing, such as trail-
ers or mobile homes, might be said to have customers rather than
clients. The form, production, and delivery of these houses are all
completely standardized (meaning there are no surprises for the
consumer), with the end product sold essentially as a consumer
good through distribution channels not unlike those of automobiles or other durables. The product in the form of manufactured
housing, although considered to be at the low end of the housing
continuum, does have many advantages, including affordability,
ease of transportation facilitated by the integration of the house
on the chassis, and off-site factory inspection, which circumvents
local performance codes. The viability of the trailer/manufactured
house has recently attracted architects to lend their expertise to
this component of the housing market.

Nevertheless, evoking a different picture entirely is the
word *client*, which implies a give-and-take working relationship
between design producer and design consumer. Consider the traditional model, in which an individual architect works directly with a
single client to design a unique result perfectly suited to the client.
As a licensed professional, the architect provides not a product
but a service, acting as the agent for the client in navigating the
complex maze of construction. The resulting constructed object,
likely executed by a similarly specialized custom house builder,
is as custom in its execution as int design, lovingly assembled by
craftspeople.

These two ends of the continuum bracket the following
examination of four makers of housing whose work illuminates how
changes in digital production extend the reach of the architect's
influence. In these models, the target market for architectural
design ranges from bespoke client to end consumer, and the fabrication strategies either support traditional construction methods
or look to reinvent building assembly itself. The resulting artifact
is delivered to the market to satisfy varying aspirations for both
quality and market reach. In each example, computer technology
transforms some part of the delivery process, but that contribution
is of a different character in each case and the marketing and
positioning strategies vary accordingly.

Consumers' growing insistence on good design is apparent
in the brisk sales of products sold by companies like Target and
IKEA. And so, in responding to the demands for affordable housing
in Sweden, contractor Skanska partnered with IKEA to create the
BoKlok housing system, which meets the needs of small families.
The goal was to develop a well-designed "housing product"
while taking advantage of IKEA's manufacturing and production
values. BoKlok "chose an unconventional approach" from the very

beginning of their process, analyzing the needs of the consumers within their market and carefully positioning their product:

Instead of calling in an architect, the company contacted Statistics Sweden and asked, "What is the current composition of households in this country?" In 1996, 75 percent of house-holds in large towns and cities were one, two, or three-person households....These small households have different require-ments in the home to those on the "second-hand" or used house market....BoKlok chose to focus on this segment and began to investigate the disposable income of small households....Top of the list was a desire to live in secure, small-scale surroundings. Other wishes included a desire to live close to the countryside, with good relations to one's neighbors, ideally with a little garden and a gate to close. It was also important to have a home that was light, well-planned, functional, and furnished with natural materials.[1]

By 2006 BoKlok had produced five thousand affordable apartment in Sweden. The units are essentially identical in design (the exterior siding differs among developments), and occupants receive a stipend to furnish and decorate with IKEA products. BoKlok has positioned its housing in a marketplace already familiar with the value-priced, attractive designs that IKEA offers. The houses themselves—two units prefabricated by heavily computerized manufacturing processes by means of computerized production processes that are then trucked to the site to form an apartment—are entirely a product solution, not unlike a coffee table. The apart-ments are leased long term or rented directly from IKEA stores, making ease of "purchase" part of the appeal. Like most other IKEA products, which suggest design intent but do not identify the designer, BoKlok caters to consumers who do not need or even want a customized individualized product.[2]

In the United States, consumer demand is met in the form of the hundreds of thousands of units built each year by production house builders—like KB Home, Pulte Homes, and Standard Pacific Homes—who build almost 25 percent of all housing in the United States. The sheer number of units that these companies build suggests that they have found the "sweet spot" where consumer demand, production effectiveness, and construction scale meet. They exploit the efficiency of standardized, adaptable plans with

1 Ewa Magnassum, BoKlock, Lecture at Yale University, 10/27/2006

2 There are exceptions to this, as certain products sold at IKEA have small signs with

the name and image of the designer of a particular product displayed in front of it. As letting the buyer believe that IKEA is a fam-ily of caring individuals than with promoting

a strategy, it seems to be more related to

"star" designers, such as Martha Stewart with Kmart or Michael Graves with Target.

Ikea Boklok house

Ikea Boklok house
interior.

limited customization to give purchasers a sense of buying a customized product—the "touch of an architect" (but as with IKEA, no designer is named) without the associated investment in time, trouble, or fees.

In 2007, before the housing market began its downturn, Standard Pacific generated approximately 10,000 units annually from 1,500 standard plans. And while the company's customers are aware that their dream house is derived from a standard plan, Standard Pacific offers enough customization through its enormous database of plans, fixtures, and finishes to satisfy buyers' individual requirements and accommodate the particular locale. Using complex data structures, assembly routines, and digital models, Standard Pacific delivers design quality by providing the appearance of design choice through computational brute force, replacing an individualized design process with a large menu of options. By limiting the range of these options within a given development, they drive down costs through construction repetition, building standard blocks of stick-frame construction three hundred units at a time.

By standardizing the fit and furnishing of these houses, Standard Pacific hopes to protect the perception that their houses are customized while increasing the efficiency of their delivery to the marketplace. They operate at a scale that benefits from thousands of consumer responses in the form of configured houses, and they use that data to relentlessly refine the subsequent products and record those decisions in the configuration database.

Ikea Boklok prefabri-
cated house section
being lifted into
place, 2007

This is stick-built construction at its most ruthlessly efficient, with Standard Pacific striving for more standardization and predictability without sacrifice of market position.

American architect Charlie Lazor is a co-founder of Blu Dot, a "flat-packed" modular furniture designer and manufacturer. Through this venture he and his partners, like designers at IKEA, learned the aesthetic sensibilities and production strategies made available by computer-controlled manufacture of components and the logic of their proportions, connections, and shipping configurations. Blu Dot targets a higher-end market than IKEA, however, by attaching Lazor's own design identity to the brand. He extended his knowledge to his current work with a housing product he calls "FlatPak," which Lazor characterizes as "using the philosophies of Blu Dot at the scale of [a] dwelling." An eight-foot gridded modular panel system—the system packs flat, unlike BoKlok's preassembled room units—is attached to a frame of predetermined dimensional variety, and clients/customers are offered choices of panel color and unit width, height, and length. Like Blu Dot, FlatPak embraces the idea of using a predetermined kit of tectonic parts and combines this attitude with an inclination toward customized architecture that requires the deft hand of the architect to come to fruition. Lazor sees the shape limitations and the panelized aesthetic as part of the appeal of this prefabricated product; as with the brand loyalty created by car manufacturers—the attachment to Audis, for example—the consumer takes as much pleasure in the standardized, recognizable aesthetic as in a particular color

Lazor Office, FlatPak
Matrix, Value as Organizational Concept, 2006

FlatPak: Matrix

Value as organizational concept

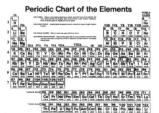

Periodic Chart of the Elements

FlatPak Wall Panel Matrix

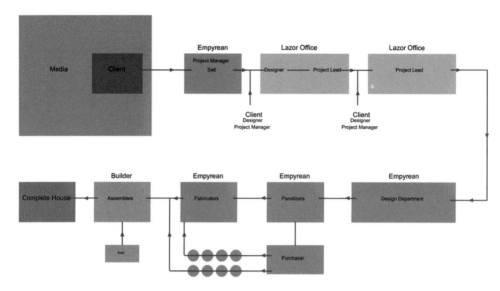

choice. Lazor aspires to the mid-market—consumers with architect-designed sensibilities but of modest means. One concludes
that Lazor therefore wishes to tap into a broader pool of potential
clients but has no wish to spread his influence to a greater number
of finished projects.

At the high end of the house design continuum is the
mass-customized Loblolly House. Designers KieranTimberlake
use a design strategy derived from analogous approaches in the
automobile industry (a reduction in the number of joints, a coalesc-
ing of mechanical systems into modules or "chunks" that are
limited only by the need to be standardized at the point of joinery)
to increase the customization and individuation of each house
they create. Unlike the philosophy that guides Lazor's FlatPak,
KieranTimberlake believe that the success of prefabrication rests
on masking its standardized origins and achieving full individuation of the chunks. In the case of the Loblolly House, the infinite
choices of skin and framing shape, standardized only at the joinery
of member to member and skin to member, maximize the opportunities for differentiation within the logic of prefabrication. The
computer-controlled design that is also used by IKEA, Standard
Pacific, and FlatPak is stretched farther by KieranTimberlake in service of design control, not just construction control. The resulting
product—constructed in this case in less than six weeks—achieves
its aim of bespoke, individualized design without pretense to mass-
market appeal but rather as a theory of production and assembly
strategy. Although the final cost of the project was not made
public, and so the economic implications of the process cannot be

<
Lazor Office, workflow
chart for FlatPak
house, 2006

>
Lazor Office, FlatPak
under construction,
2006

Lazor Office, completed FlatPak House, 2007

Kieran Timberlake,
fabricator working on
panel for Loblolly
House, 2006

completely understood, the appeal of the Loblolly House approach to subsequent clients is the efficiency and predictability of the construction technique and a design process that can still lay claim to architectural authorship. The idea of mass customization asserts that individual tastes can be accommodated for a broader spectrum of tastes, completely inverting the BoKlok strategy. In this project it was a technique for the architect to exert control over the final product rather than as a means of taking that product to scale in the marketplace of customers looking for housing or of redefining the relationship of the architect to that market.

What do these four models indicate about how designers, tempted by digital capabilities and manufacturing efficiencies, choose their clients/customers (marketing) and explain their capabilities (positioning)? While both KieranTimberlake and Lazor look to manufactured efficiency to address a small number of clients (the number the firms can handle in individual relationships) the essence of BoKlok's strategy is mass adoption through the efficiencies of replacing individual design choice with design dictated by market research on a targeted demographic. FlatPak and Loblolly House press manufactured production in the service of greater design control for individual architects and clients (since architectural intervention is required for each project). At the same time, FlatPak, like BoKlok, is willing to conflate design quality with brand (IKEA), although IKEA's branding is seemingly unauthored while FlatPak's is decidedly not.

Standard Pacific and similar production house builders are working both sides of this equation against the middle. They

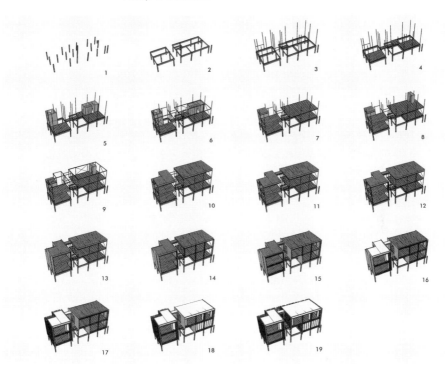

Kieran Timberlake, 19 phases of Loblolly House assembly, 2006

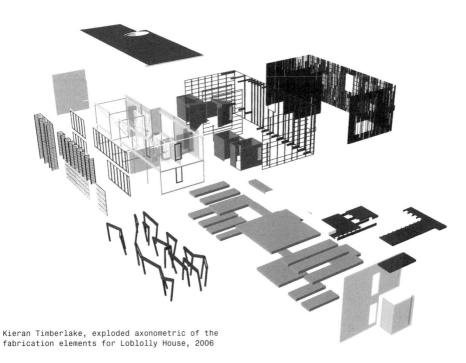

Kieran Timberlake, exploded axonometric of the
fabrication elements for Loblolly House, 2006

want the perception of custom design but the ability to reach the broadest possible market by improving the means of both design (via databases and digital design configurators) and production (with manufactured components like prefabricated frames and cabinetry)—without the need for an individual architect. Indeed, they have the market reach, capitalization, and distribution channels necessary to achieve this end and establish market standards (and customer expectations) at a scale unmatched by the other three examples. Like IKEA, and unlike FlatPak and Loblolly, they do this "author free."

It is this seemingly irreconcilable tension—between market penetration made possible by highly repeatable digital procedures in design and production versus the positioning of "architect-designed" products and services—that architects themselves must resolve in the future as housing and other building types are increasingly created with automated processes. In one scenario, the raw efficiencies of digitally created designs aligned with powerful manufacturing processes and their accompanying market-distribution channels will empower architects and design to spread their influence widely (and, it is assumed, improve the resulting buildings). Imagine James Timberlake in control of the machinery that is Standard Pacific. But at this point, no architect of such reputation finds him- or herself with that kind of influence. In another, less encouraging but more likely scenario, manufacturing methodologies tied tightly to product distribution strategies designed to optimize market penetration supplant architectural design at the head of the supply chain, thereby losing the potential potency of mass customization to design automation. Loss of control over individual results in order to reach a larger market is the price that may have to be paid to avoid this fate unless architects are willing to automate not just the means of manufacturing but design itself.

Models for Practice:
Past, Present, Future
Phillip G. Bernstein

Various contributors to this book argue for transformation in the design-to-construction process and for dramatic changes in the creation and execution of design. Yet large-scale adjustments to practice models and radical innovations in business process structure are infrequent in the architecture/engineering/construction (AEC) industry, since innovation is constrained by concerns over liability, intellectual property, or even the appropriate division of labor.[1]

Coinciding with the explosion in the use of digital technologies and techniques, however, is what appears to be a radical transformation in the industry, driven not only by the availability of these new tools but by broader influences as well.[2] A key inspiration is the lingering dysfunction of the construction process, well understood to have, in the main, missed the productivity gains of the late-twentieth century made possible in other industries by digital techniques. Modern construction often fails to achieve even the simplest schedule, budget, or performance objectives, and research suggests that as much as 30 percent of construction costs are wasted by inefficient construction processes, inadequate design documentation, poorly managed supply chains, and dangerous field conditions.[3] Another motivating force is that designers' and constructors' profit margins—which waver between 3 percent and 15 percent on average, depending on economic conditions—do not adequately reflect the risks inherent in building. And finally, as the end of the first decade of the twenty-first century approaches, expectations for more environmentally responsible buildings rise, yet AEC industry processes can hardly support yet another performance objective added to the list of project expectations.

The failure of architects, engineers, and contractors to define or achieve prescribed outcomes with consistency might be ascribed to the Fordian linear process that characterizes traditional design: the phases of schematic design through construction administration that are the frames of AEC business instruments like contracts, insurance, schedules, and invoices.[4] That structure is based in part on the hierarchical nature of the design process (where the architect subcontracts its responsibilities to other professionals and trades) and on the further separation of the acts of "thinking" and "making" required to execute a completed building.

1   See Ashcraft, "Furthering Collaboration"; Noble, "Controlling Intellectual Property"; and Martin, "Postscript," all in this volume.

2   Taylor, "Innovation Rates and Project Network Organization."

3   "New Wiring," The Economist, Jan 13, 2000.

4   See Deamer, "Detail Deliberations" in this volume.

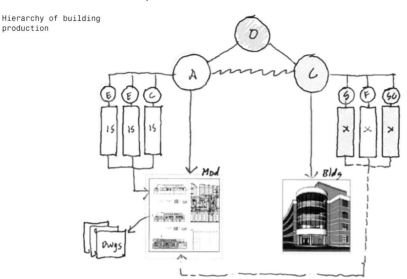

Under that classic organizational structure, the architect ("A") is contracted to the owner ("O") as its agent to provide a professional service, design, that is empowered by the state under professional registration law. Sometime later, the constructor ("C") will be contracted to provide the built product. Here, the architect provides "thinking" services: exercising judgment and representing ideas in the form of abstract diagrams, words, and charts that are transmitted to the owner and contractor in the form of what are known as the instruments of service. The primary role of the architect is to think about the design and certify that thought process by virtue of his or her professional stamp on the final product. Considerations of how the building is to be built—the "making"— are delegated explicitly to the constructor, whose responsibilities include determining the means and methods for accomplishing the design. The architect is not to be involved in these means and methods because that is not part of the process of thinking about design. The constructor is not to be involved in the creation of the design, because he or she lacks the professional standing to do so and thus arrives only after the completion of the design.[5]

In fact, the most significant single transaction in this relationship is the transmission of the working drawings (instruments of service) to the constructor (who was likely not involved in their preparation), since the "thinkers" provide instructions

5   AIA Contracts B101-2007 and A201-2007 delineate specifically that the architect does not have responsibility for such means and methods and that the contractor must rely on the professional certifications of the architect to determine the design intent represented in the contract documents.

to the "makers." Construction insight is wholly missing from the conceptualization of the design, and design insight is applied only sparingly during its execution. Further, detailed instructions for the assembly of the building itself will be left to a later effort, shop drawings, in which specific fabricators will document their detailed intentions for approval by the original designers, whose original designs included only glimmers of the information truly needed to make the design real.

Attempts to close this gap between intention and execution are at the root of current innovation catalyzed by the more extensive use of digital tools and processes. Along with the diffusion of desktop computing power, digital fabrication methodologies, high-resolution displays, and the interconnectivity created by the internet comes a wide variety of representational and collaborative tools available to the entire AEC supply chain. The so-called digital revolution as manifest in the AEC industry found firm footing in the early 1990s, with digital technology being used for computerized drafting (AutoCAD), 3-D rendering and visualization, and numerical modeling (Excel). Today the proliferation of personal computers, the distribution potential provided by the internet, and the dramatic increase in processing power, storage, and display resolution have inspired the widespread, but still discontinuous, application of digital tools to various AEC processes.

A diagram that Skidmore, Owings & Merrill (SOM) created to map the relationships of software used by their New York office proves useful in assessing the changes that digital technology has wrought in the industry. The diagram does not just organize the software deployed to complete a design, it depicts the social organization of the office itself: the design, technical production, and construction "departments" are clearly legible. Of particular interest are the clusters of tools assigned to various sections of the SOM workflow— sketch information model to conceptual design, building information model to technical production, and so forth. Where there was once a single drafting platform that created the foundational design document—the analog drawing—we now have billions of bytes of design data forming a loose coalition of application datasets. At one time, AEC storage mechanisms consisted of filing cabinets and flat files, with the physical size of the images determining the use of one over the other. Now information resides on a computer server in the office, in a wide variety of disconnected formats.

The SOM diagram is emblematic of more than just a data management challenge. It also makes apparent that the transition from computerized drafting platforms to this smorgasbord of tools is part of a broader shift in the relationship between design

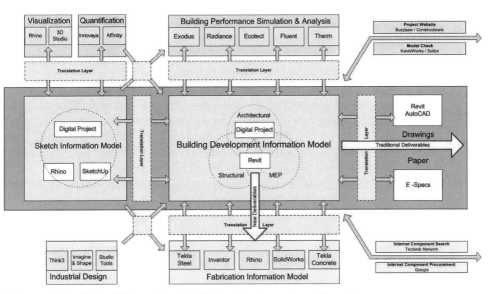

Skidmore, Owings & Merrill's mapping of relationship of computer software to users

and construction. While many of the new digital tools support traditional form exploration and depiction that might otherwise have been done in sketch or physical model, others provide opportunities to control the means of construction and fabrication or to predict the behavior of the design in advance of engineering analysis or construction, results that can only be attained digitally. SOM is taking greater control over the final product of design, and thereby breaking down the traditional barriers between "thinking" and "making"—barriers that originated in the definition of architectural practice in the early twentieth century and were ossified by the project delivery methods, standards of care, and contract models that characterized the practice of architecture by century's end. Through its efforts, SOM is conflating intention and execution, blurring the distinction between them.

But the fundamental transformation in the means of design representation is only hinted at by the SOM taxonomy. While the passage from analog drawing with pencils and drafting instruments to computer-aided drafting felt momentous at the time it occurred, it was actually a mere translation of hand drawing to computerized drawing; the end results were identical if more precise, and little change of process resulted. Design representation is now moving from drawing-based methods to model-based methods, from computer-aided drafting to building information modeling (BIM). Like precedent methods in manufacturing,

AEC representation is now moving from loosely connected, orthographic abstractions of designs (drawings) to behaviorally accurate, 3-D digital prototypes of designs that include extensive metadata which can be used for analysis and evaluation. Drawings become not an end product of the design process but "reports" from a model. Dynamic, parametric design representations can be the basis of optimization, high-resolution virtual walk-throughs that provide the designer with significant insight during the design process.

The parametric results of design representation, which expose geometry, metadata descriptors of that geometry, relationships, and inferential conclusions about the design generated by analysis algorithms, will reconstitute the instrument of service, replacing the 2-D, analog version. Eventually, that digital information will link directly to computer-controlled fabrication devices, closing the intention-execution gap thoroughly and eliminating the need for traditional construction documents entirely.

The motivations are apparent and the tools are evolving rapidly, but the underlying business models need to continue to change to make further process improvements possible. In particular, adjustment is necessary in the historically asymmetrical relationship between architects and their clients, with a recentering such that the benefits of the putative improvements in process accrue to the designer. But if architects define those benefits only in terms of formal or aesthetic ends, they will miss the fundamental and unique opportunity offered by the transition. Closing the intention-execution gap, bridging the acts of "thinking" and "making," will also be driven as much by clients' desire to increase productivity and achieve more predictable outcomes, so business models that rely more closely on collaboration between thinkers and makers, designers and constructors, architects and engineers, can be tied to results. Current prescriptive business models venerate lowest first cost fixed fees and standard form contracts. In alternative "integrated" delivery approaches, risks and rewards are a function of measurable outcomes defined at the outset of a project, and success or failure is attributed to the entire AEC team rather than to a single participant.[6] The potential rewards of success therefore can be reaped not only by the biggest spender (the constructor) but also to the designer, whose insights (and resulting deliverables) drove the result from the outset. Everyone wins, or everyone loses.

6   AIA Contract Documents Committee and the AIA California Council, "Integrated Project Delivery: A Guide," AIA, http://www.aia.org/contractdocs/AIAS077630.

Thus, new methods of digital representation, associated changes in business process, restructured project relationships made possible by these concepts, and the coherent execution of design itself all are profitable to the project, and so each of the participants profits accordingly. In such a model, designers embrace risk beyond the design concept in exchange for both aesthetic and financial reward. Orchestrating these tools and integrating them into the new process—defining "craft" as both process design and material effects—drives both agendas.[7]

Questions posed about how these innovations take place often center on decisions about control: who is in charge of the design process? Who controls the building information model? Who is assigned blame in case of technical failures? But these questions derive from years of patterned behavior based on traditional AEC business models and are largely irrelevant in integrated, digitally based projects where intention and execution are deeply connected. Business calculations in construction projects are frequently computed as zero sum, meaning that one party benefits at the expense of another, creating classes of winners and losers for each building project. Can the architect shoehorn his or her ideas into the budget? Can the contractor be convinced to build as much as possible under its hard bid? But in collaborative models that combine responsibilities, risks, and rewards, and that provide open to access to information, disputes over control give way to issues of leadership: who is best suited to make a decision that benefits the project itself? Control then moves dynamically between members of the integrated team.

Research on the dynamics of collaboration suggests that slavish focus on winning to the exclusion of overall community good is a short-lived strategy that provides intensive but limited reward to the winner, who loses out in the longer term.[8] In *The Evolution of Cooperation* game theorist Robert Axelrod tested the proposition that the most effective collaboration strategy is to reciprocate cooperation without exception but to retaliate immediately against defections from collaboration, thus rewarding cooperation. Over a long time horizon, such a strategy inevitably results in the greatest potential benefit to all participants in a decision-making system.

Axelrod's insights can be applied usefully to process innovation in the AEC industry, and various contributors to this book make many other suggestions. But how do such innovations become widely adopted in the industry and get diffused among all

7 See Marble, "Imagining Risk," and Kolarevic, "The Craft of Digital Making," both in this volume.

8 See Robert M. Axelrod, *The Evolution of Collaboration* (revised edition) (New York: Basic Books, 1984).

the roles, responsibilities, and relationships that constitute it? What makes innovations like building information modeling or integrated project delivery stick sufficiently so that the resulting changes benefit all parts of the industry supply chain?

Silicon Valley technologist Geoffrey Moore suggests that the diffusion of innovation occurs in predicable patterns and that new ideas are first adopted by a very small but motivated group of technology enthusiasts who are energized by the idea of innovation for change's sake.[9] These "innovators" are rapidly followed by a group of "early adopters" who look to the innovators to solve problems for which they otherwise can find no answers. SOM's panoply of technological platforms, for example, suggests not unbridled enthusiasm but rather the desire to use digital tools to improve productivity and produce results that cannot be achieved in any other way. SOM is one of the first to cross Moore's "chasm," the period of time when the balance of the market watches to see if they succeed or fail. And that success will proceed not just from the formal boldness and aesthetic innovation of their design work but from changes to their business processes and financial benefit.[10] While their competitors watch, the early adopters of intentional execution reset the boundaries of process.

Yet individual examples of success do not necessarily create repeatable artifacts, and the industry's recent hunger for innovative structures (and the descriptive contracts, standards, and protocols that must accompany them) will take time to satisfy. The civil engineer Henry Petroski asserts that truly useful things take care and intensive iteration to perfect.[11] Today's fork evolved over hundreds of years of refinement; the modern zipper took more than twenty years to perfect into something reliable and reproducible. The ideas that will reconstitute design, combining intention and execution, will need to be repeated, refined, and perfected in the changing environments in which buildings are built. Vincent Scully once asserted that architecture requires both innovators and clarifiers to progress. Eliminating the lingering dysfunction of the building process will require both.

9   See Geoffrey Moore, Crossing the Chasm: Marketing and Selling High-Tech Products to Mainstream Customers (revised edition), (New York: Harper Collins Publishers, 1999).

10 See Sharples, "Information Technology and the Changing Structure of Labor" in this volume.

11 See Henry Petroski, The Evolution of Useful: How Everyday Artifacts from Forks and Pints to Paper Clips and Zippers— Came to Be as They Are (New York: Vintage Books, 1994).

Postscript
Reinhold Martin

I want to begin with a story.

In 1991 I took the Architectural Registration Exam (ARE) in New York. It was organized slightly differently than it is now, with a more overt emphasis on macho endurance. You had to do it all in one week, one section after the other, lined up in military formation with your fellow architects-to-be (or not-to-be) in the Fifty-seventh Street piers—a spectacle I will never forget. The climax, which was misnamed "Building Design" and took place on the last day, amounted to a race to see who could "design" the worst possible suburban strip mall in something like eight hours. In those predigital days, you brought your portable drawing board with you. These drawing boards were talismanic artifacts—passed down from one intern to the other within and between offices, where it was hoped that whatever magic had enabled the previous owner to pass the exam (and therefore no longer be in need of the drawing board) would remain attached to the object as it entered your hands. Magic aside, however, the ARE was a kind of industrialized hazing ritual that translated the social elitism of what the nineteenth century called a "gentleman's profession" into a test to see who was still standing at the end of hell week. With the advent of computers and flexible scheduling, the exam has probably become more civilized, and I would like to think that, in turn, the profession has become less macho, though of this I cannot be sure.

In any event, the first section of the ARE, which still exists in more or less the same form, was called "Pre-Design." Among the knowledge tested in this section was a token knowledge of architectural history and theory. Yes, theory, in the form of multiple-choice questions. And so when I took the exam it included this question, worded in exactly this beautiful way: "What kind of symmetry did Gropius's teachings teach?" Although I had studied a bit of architectural history and theory myself by that time (I had a degree in it from the Architectural Association), I did not know the answer to this question. I had to guess. Somehow, I still passed the exam. And thenceforth I was officially authorized to use the word *architect* after my name.

But I was so puzzled by this question of Gropius's symmetry (and by the possibility that the National Council of Architectural Registration Boards [NCARB] knew something I did not), that I decided to do a Ph.D. As it turns out, that did not help much. In fact, in many ways it seemed to lead further away from NCARB and from architectural practice entirely. And so on the poster for the conference upon which this book is based I found myself described not as an "architect" but as a "theorist," who somewhat mysteriously remains a partner in an architectural practice. That practice has in turn been called "theoretical," probably because we do not really build anything, and what we do do, we often do not get paid for. (This is a reasonable definition of theoretical architecture, really: architecture you do not get paid for. I suspect that many of you are also theoretical architects.)

In the old days, the kind of architecture I have done, which exists mainly in digital form, would have been called "paper architecture," its dignity thus preserved by association with at least some kind of materiality, if only the lowly materiality of paper (or cardboard, as the case may be). But unlike earlier paper architects, it is not because I somehow object to the immorality of the profession that I do not build—after all, it is no more immoral than teaching. I do not build because I do not have time to build. I am too busy thinking about architecture, all the time. And according to certain narratives regarding the transformation of "work" in the so-called digital age, thought is a form of production. Indeed, to note how thought itself was industrialized in the early part of the twentieth century, I need only mention the slogan that used to be affixed to the photographs of Thomas Watson Sr. in old IBM advertisements: "Think." Whereas, to underline the newer, postmodern ways in which such thought—or really, the image of thought—has been converted into the currency of the postindustrial age, we need only remember the slogan that has long been affixed to IBM's upstart competitor, Apple: "Think Different."

It would follow, then, that architects in the digital age should be more like thinkers. In recognition of this possibility, it is worth noting that in any case, architects do not build buildings. Builders build buildings. This is called a division of labor, and it has been in place for a long time. Still, it is quite possible that the specific ways in which architects do not build buildings today are relatively new. In 1992 (a year after I took the ARE) the economist Robert Reich, who would later become Bill Clinton's secretary of labor, gave architects a new job description: he called them "symbolic analysts." Actually, he just listed architects along with other symbolic analysts, like advertising executives, marketing strategists, art directors, writers, research scientists, engineers, and even university professors. According to Reich, "symbolic analysts solve, identify, and broker problems by manipulating symbols. They simplify reality into abstract images that can be rearranged, juggled, experimented with, communicated to other specialists, and then, eventually, transformed back into reality."[1]

Others would call the work performed by symbolic analysts a form of "immaterial labor." In the division of labor associated with

1   Reich, Robert B. *The Work of Nations: Preparing Ourselves for 21st Century*   *Capitalism* (New York: Vintage Books, 1991), 178.

globalization, immaterial labor is analytical, communicative, and often creative work done with abstractions, generally (though not exclusively) within the so-called service sector of the global economy, and increasingly with the help of computers. The ARE tests for an ability to perform a particular type of immaterial labor. This takes the form of work involving the manipulation of symbols, be they moment diagrams, occupancy charts contained in building codes, or the symbolic language of architecture itself (and thus the question, "What kind of symmetry did Gropius's teachings teach?"). In the late 1990s, the exam itself began to make use of computers, a development that—parallel academic experiments with computers notwithstanding—I would argue marks a key moment in the transformation of architectural practice in the United States into full-fledged immaterial labor, with the talismanic computer taking the place of the talismanic drawing board.

In this context the production of architecture occurs at three interrelated levels: the production of objects (i.e., manufacturing and logistics), the production of signs (i.e., symbolic analysis), and the production of experience, or affect. As dimensions of immaterial labor, these can be further distinguished by the different sites in which they occur. Immaterial manufacturing can be defined as the continuous, computerized incorporation of external data into the fabrication process, as in mass customization. This usually occurs "in the field," as they say—which today is very often no longer a field but a robotic factory supported by an immense logistical infrastructure. Immaterial analysis can be defined as the production, communication, and synthesis in and between the offices of the architect and his or her so-called consultants of the same (or other) data—environmental data, structural data, social data, formal data, and so on. In other words, design. The third type of immaterial labor—affective labor—describes the kind of work that both architect and architecture do at an emotional level, through the production of experiences. They do this work person to person or building to person—as image (circulating in publications, etc.), as persona (the starchitect, etc.), and as supposedly direct experience (when the building is finally built).

Computers participate in and enable all three of these levels, as well as their interaction. But, just as it passed from the drawing board to the computer, talismanic status now seems to be passing to the "new machines"—that is, CNC machines, waterjet cutters, 3-D printers, and so on—that, with the help of human operators, physically perform the work of immaterial manufacture. Access to such machines is increasingly considered a decisive factor in the production of cutting-edge design, as perhaps it should be. Still, the new preoccupation with the new machines does strike

me as slightly fetishistic. I do not really mean fetishistic at the level
of "boys' toys" (after all, girls can have fetishes too). I mean fetishistic at the level of religion—remembering that a fetish is, technically
and historically, a religious object. And oddly enough, what I think
is being fetishized in all the talk about new techniques is not the
materiality of the machines themselves as very cool pieces of
hardware (they are actually kind of clunky), or even the materiality
of the building components coming out of them. What I think is
being fetishized is exactly the opposite: the supposed immaterial-
ity of immaterial labor.

Time and again it is announced, with religious conviction,
that computer-driven production is leading us to a new materialism, but nothing, it seems to me, could be farther from the truth.
Yes, the new techniques may seem to lead us back to modernism:
back to a concern with new forms of construction and back to new
materials, which are now warehoused online in colorful places
with colorful names like Material ConneXion, instead of in "dark,
satanic" steel mills. At times, they even seem to lead back to the
love affair with the assembly line, now populated by sexy robots
in place of shadowy, machinelike workers. But above all, the
so-called new materialism betrays what can be called a transparency fetish: a devotion to what the revolutionary architect/artist
El Lissitzky used to call "immaterial materiality," meaning a kind
of magic, virtual object produced with physical processes. The
difference today is, sadly, that transparency stands not as a figure
for freedom, truth, or at least enlightened reason, as it did for Lissitzky and so many other modernists: today transparency means—
precisely—darkness, control, and myth.

Allow me to explain. Under the regime of mass customization, symbolic analysis, and the "experience" industry, the
designer's preferred motto is WYSIWYG, What You See Is What
You Get, which represents a kind of mystified transparency. Look
at the complex forms on your computer screen: those are exactly
what you will see when the thing is built. The software/hardware
assemblage called computer-aided design/computer-aided manufacturing will be able to translate—directly and seamlessly—just
those forms into 3-D built space, with minimal interference from
inconvenient rigidities, like magic. The ideal therefore seems to
be a cognitive and productive transparency, based on noise-free
communication the feedback loops of which enable just-in-time
flexibility and an absolute responsiveness, all within a horizon of
infinite possibility—a variability without end.

Fine. But to produce new architecture is not just to produce
new objects: it is also to produce new subjects. And so, in the case
of mass customization, for example, a potentially infinite array of

objects that pose new problems for designers (take, for example, the infamous "halting problem," proven unsolvable by computer scientist Alan Turing) also suggests a potentially infinite array of subjects. In this light, the term *mass* in *mass customization* is misleading, since the individualized postmodern subjects of mass-customized architecture are precisely *not* the anonymous modern subjects of mass-produced architecture as imagined by architects such as, say, Mies or Hilberseimer. Instead they are, like their objects, each a little different, requiring so-called nonstandard design techniques to accommodate their nonstandard lives. In short, as distinct from the modernist masses, the subject produced by the regime of production known as mass customization must now be called a "person."

But who, really, is this person, this supposedly "free" individual with an individual personality and individual needs? In the old days, another name for the prototypical subject of mass production was the "worker": the standardized subject of an assembly line making standardized objects. Today another name for the prototypical subject, or person, of mass customization is the "consumer." But if the theme of this book is concerned with the effects of new forms of production, and if the consumer is the prototypical subject, or agent, of the new means of production, what then do consumers actually produce? Well, technically, nothing. They simply consume. And to the relief of many, this activity stands in sharp contrast to that of the "worker" who, historically, was thought to have been capable of producing quite a bit, including—according to some—a revolution. By contrast, it seems pretty difficult to imagine consumers producing a revolution, other than the much-vaunted "consumer revolutions" that are regularly announced with the arrival of each new marketing technique and each new product.

This is what the new transparency fetishism conceals, with its regular announcements of revolutionary new techniques for producing revolutionary new objects. It conceals the fact that very little, if anything, is actually being produced that is new. Instead, in perfect postmodern acquiescence, too much of the rhetoric surrounding the new machines, new forms of teamwork, and new professional arrangements misrecognizes reproduction for production. That is, rather than producing a new, postconsumerist world inaccessible within the horizon of our television screens (as Lissitzky would have hoped), these arrangements seem all too often dedicated to reproducing the world as it already exists: a world inhabited by consumer-subjects who imagine themselves as mass-customized "persons" on a parametric sliding scale, each thinking (or really, not thinking) a little differently.

Now of course there still are actual, old-fashioned, out-sourced "workers" out there—people who build the machines that build our buildings. In fact, there are millions of them, maybe billions. And of course they are almost entirely invisible to transparency fetishists. But do not worry, what I am saying does not just come down to an earnest plea for us to attend to the plight of these actual—and actually underpaid—workers. After all, they are invisible—and what you cannot see, you cannot do much about. It is, instead, a recommendation that we attend to the blind spots built into the stories we tell ourselves about our technologies, our techniques, and the organization of our profession and of our discipline. It is a recommendation, in other words, that we attend to the nature and consequences of our own work with greater precision.

Going back to the ARE once again, and to that impossible question about Gropius's symmetries, the multiple-choice answer that I chose was an oxymoron: "asymmetrical symmetry." Whether it was the right answer or not, I still do not know. But I have to admit that it has become one of my favorite concepts, since in the ancien régime that preceded the modern one, symmetry, with all its authoritarian overtones, nevertheless opened a path to enlightened reason, with its logic of part to whole, of this to that. It was, in that sense, the architectural predecessor of transparency, which in mass-produced modernism made the light of reason literal (think here of the Bauhaus building itself). Only a postmodernist (or maybe even a poststructuralist) working at NCARB at the cusp of the age of mass customization could possibly have imagined the disorienting figure of an asymmetrical symmetry. But perhaps this asymmetrical symmetry is, after all, a secret partner of Lissitzky's idea of immaterial materiality—a paradoxical property of paradoxical objects that may yet correspond to paradoxical subjects—hardly easy, hardly seamless, hardly transparent.

In any event, the work that I do now, fifteen years after being authorized by NCARB to use the word architect after my name, is largely academic—it is, in other words, the work of a symbolic analyst. Of that, a significant portion involves reflecting on, revising, and reinventing the kinds of stories our discipline tells itself under the sign of "history." So it is heartening, but also disturbing, to see that fifteen years later, NCARB still requires a token knowledge of architectural history as a condition for admission into the profession of architecture. Among its recommended references for the Pre-Design section of the ARE are Kenneth Frampton's *Modern Architecture: A Critical History*, and (of all things) Sir Banister Fletcher's *A History of Architecture*, to say nothing of various New Urbanist manifestos. But asymmetrical symmetry aside, perhaps the most relevant question here—in response to which histories have yet to be written—has to do with the assumptions about historical progress and historical change that are made by the techno-deterministic (if not techno-triumphalist) version of history celebrated by transparency fetishists. In other words, what—specifically—is the historicity of our supposedly "new" machines, "new" materials, and "new" forms of organization? Where have they come from and—more important—where are they going? On these and so many other questions, there is work to be done.

Contributors'
Biographies /
Index / Image
Credits

Howard W. Ashcraft Jr. is a senior partner at the San Francisco law firm of Hanson, Bridgett, Marcus, Vlahos & Rudy, LLP, where he specializes in construction law infrastructure and project delivery. He is a fellow of the American College of Construction Lawyers, a former governing committee member of the American Bar Association's Forum on the Construction Industry, and an arbitrator in the American Arbitration Association's Large and Complex Program.

Phillip G. Bernstein is a vice president at Autodesk, Inc., where he is responsible for technology strategy for the company's architectural, engineering, and construction software. Previously he was an associate principal at Cesar Pelli & Associates in New Haven, Connecticut, where he coordinated overall project management. Bernstein is a fellow of the American Institute of Architects and former chair of the organization's National Documents Committee.

James Carpenter is the principal of the New York–based design practice James Carpenter Design Associates Inc. The firm specializes in the use of glass, and 7 World Trade Center and Times Warner Center are among its architecture projects. Carpenter received the MacArthur Fellowship Award in 2004, and a monograph of his work—James Carpenter: Environmental Refractions, by Sandro Marpillero—was published by Birkhäuser / Princeton Architectural Press in 2007.

Peggy Deamer is principal of Deamer Studio, based in Brooklyn, New York. From 1986 to 2002 she was a partner in the architectural firm of Deamer + Phillips. She is a professor of architecture at Yale University, where she served as associate academic dean from 2002 to 2006. She headed the School of Architecture and Planning of the University of Auckland in 2007. Deamer is the author of The Millennium House: Peggy Deamer Seminar and Studio, 2000–2001, Yale School of Architecture (Yale School of Architecture / Monacelli Press, 2005) and co-editor of Re-Reading Perspecta: The First Fifty Years of the Yale Architectural Journal (Yale School of Architecture / MIT Press, 2006).

Kenneth Frampton is Ware Professor of Architecture at Columbia University, where he has been a faculty member since 1972. He has written numerous books, including Modern Architecture: A Critical History (4th ed., Thames & Hudson, 2007) and Studies in Tectonic Culture (MIT Press, 2001). While he was on the faculty of the Institute of Architecture and Urban Studies in New York, he co-founded the publication Oppositions.

Mark Goulthorpe began his architecture career in the office of Richard Meier, then worked as a digital design consultant to Foster + Partners in London. In 1991 he established dECOi atelier, an interior design, architecture, and urban planning practice. Goulthorpe has taught at MIT since 2003 and received a Rotch Travelling Scholarship for his studio. His work was exhibited at the Centre Pompidou in the Non-Standard Architecture show in 2007, and some of his writings have been collected in The Possibility of (an) Architecture (Routledge, 2008).

Branko Kolarevic is the Haworth Chair in Integrated Design and an associate professor of architecture at the University of Calgary. Before his appointment in Calgary, he was the Irving Distinguished Visiting Professor at Ball State University in Indiana and previously taught architecture at the University of Pennsylvania and in Hong Kong. His most recent book is Manufacturing Material Effects: Rethinking Design and Making in Architecture (Routledge, 2008), which he edited with Kevin Klinger. He is a past president of the Association for Computer Aided Design in Architecture (ACADIA) and the recipient of the ACADIA 2007 Award for Innovative Research.

Kent Larson is director of the MIT House_n Research Consortium in the MIT Department of Architecture. He also runs the MIT Open Source Building Alliance and the Changing Places research group at the MIT Media Lab. Larson practiced architecture for fifteen years in New York City in partnership with Peter L. Gluck and, more recently, as Kent Larson, Architects P.C. In 2000 his book, Louis I. Kahn: Unbuilt Masterworks (Monacelli Press), was selected as one of the ten best books in architecture by the New York Times Review of Books.

Scott Marble is a partner in the architectural practice Marble Fairbanks in New York. Since 1991 he has taught design studios at Columbia on the topics of housing and schools and was the coordinator of graduate studios from 1992 to 1994. Marble has been the editor of

Abstract, the catalog of Columbia University's Graduate School of Architecture, Planning and Preservation, since 1995, and co-edited the book *Architecture and Body* (Rizzoli, 1987). Marble was a New York Foundation for the Arts fellow in architecture in 1994, and in 1992 his firm received a Young Architects award from the Architectural League of New York.

Reinhold Martin is the director of the Temple Hoyne Buell Center in American Architecture at Columbia University and is a professor in the School of Architecture, Planning and Preservation. He is the author of *The Organizational Complex: Architecture, Media, and Corporate Space* (MIT Press, 2003) as well as a founding editor of the journal *Grey Room*. He is a partner in the firm of Martin/Baxi Architects and with Kadambari Baxi published *Entropia* (Black Dog, 2001) and *Multi-National City: Architectural Itineraries* (Actar, 2007).

Rodd Merchant is an assistant vice president with JE Dunn Construction–Rocky Mountain responsible for quality assurance and firmwide implementation of building information modeling. Previously he worked as a consulting structural engineer. Merchant also serves as vice president and treasurer of the Structural Engineers Association of Colorado and is a member of the American Institute of Steel Construction and the Associated General Contractors of America BIM Forum.

Chris Noble is a partner in the law firm of Noble & Wickersham LLP, and he specializes in the areas of design and construction. Noble is a founding fellow,

former board member, and committee chair of the American College of Construction Lawyers, a past chair of the Contract Documents Division of the American Bar Association Construction Industry Forum, and an honorary member of the Boston Society of Architects. He has taught at the Harvard Graduate School of Design and is a member of the Executive Committee of the Board of Trustees of the Boston Architectural College.

Andrew Ross is a professor and the Chair of Social and Cultural Analysis at New York University, whose research interests include labor and work; urban and suburban studies; intellectual history; social and political theory; science; ecology and technology; and cultural studies. His books include, *Fast Boat to China: Corporate Flight and the Consequences of Free Trade-Lessons from Shanghai* (Pantheon, 2006; Vintage, 2007) and *Low Pay, High Profile: The Global Push for Fair Labor* (New Press, 2004).

Kevin Rotheroe teaches at the Yale School of Architecture and runs Free Form, an architecture and sculpture studio in New York City, and Free Form Research, a nonprofit studio conducting sponsored and proprietary investigations into advanced digitally based material-forming technologies. He has received numerous fellowships and has patents on biomimetic structural systems. Previously he was an assistant professor of design at the University of Illinois at Urbana–Champaign.

Coren Sharples is a founding partner of New York–based SHoP Architects, which won the

2001 Emerging Voices Award from the Architectural League of New York, the 2001 Academy Award in Architecture from the American Academy of Arts and Letters, and a *Progressive Architecture* (P/A Award) Citation in 1999. Also, in 2000, the firm won the annual Museum of Modern Art and P.S.1 Young Architect's Program award and created the installation in the P.S.1 courtyard.

John E. Taylor is on the faculty at Columbia University and Director of the Project Network Dynamics Lab. Taylor's field research and computational simulation modeling have identified critical issues relating to project network structure that are used by industry professionals to develop and implement organizational and work-process innovation strategies. In 1996 he was awarded a Fulbright Scholarship, and he is currently an Alfred P. Sloan Foundation Industry Studies Fellow.

Paolo Tombesi teaches architectural design and practice and political economy of design at the University of Melbourne. In 2000 his "The Carriage in the Needle: Building Design and Flexible Specialization Systems" received the *Journal of Architectural Education* award for outstanding article.